New Orleans

HOME COOKING

New Orleans

HOME COOKING

DALE CURRY

PELICAN PUBLISHING COMPANY
GRETNA 2008

*The word "Pelican" and the depiction of a pelican are trademarks
of Pelican Publishing Company, Inc., and are registered in the
U.S. Patent and Trademark Office.*

Curry, Dale.
  New Orleans home cooking / by Dale Curry.
      p. cm.
  Includes index.
  ISBN 978-1-58980-519-4 (hardcover : alk. paper) 1. Cookery, American—
Louisiana style. 2. Cookery—Louisiana—New Orleans. I. Title.
  TX715.2.L68C97 2008
  641.59763'35—dc22
                              2008000221

Some recipes featured in New Orleans Home Cooking *have previously appeared in* New
Orleans Magazine *and are reprinted with the magazine's permission.*

Printed in China
Published by Pelican Publishing Company, Inc.
1000 Burmaster Street, Gretna, Louisiana 70053

To Jennifer and Elizabeth

Contents

Acknowledgments 9

Introduction 11

CHAPTER ONE
Appetizers 17

CHAPTER TWO
Soups 39

CHAPTER THREE
Salads 63

CHAPTER FOUR
Side Dishes 69

CHAPTER FIVE
Entrées 91

CHAPTER SIX
Sauces 159

CHAPTER SEVEN
Breakfast 161

CHAPTER EIGHT
Desserts 169

Index 191

Acknowledgments

Many hugs to Doug, my husband, and daughters Jennifer and Elizabeth, for their skills in cooking, tasting, and computer wizardry.

Introduction

Not the least of possessions that Hurricane Katrina swallowed up in 2005 were the cookbooks and recipe files of hundreds of thousands of residents of greater New Orleans and the Mississippi Gulf Coast. How many times have I heard the sad stories of a lost grandmother's recipe or a treasured collection of clippings? Irreplaceable. That's what they say.

Around the time that Katrina hit, I was already on the case of "lost" recipes, those not felled by waves or winds, but by—amazingly—lack of interest. Young people not cooking, too much fast food in easy reach, no time to spend in the kitchen. Thus, my goal in the food columns of *New Orleans Magazine* was to teach young people the wonders of Creole cooking, show them how to do it, and help save one of the world's greatest cuisines from the abyss of lost recipes.

Then, Katrina made it essential to combine these and other recipes into a cookbook to help keep alive the classic Creole and Cajun recipes that have taken New Orleans to legendary heights. On the menus of fine restaurants remain the great dishes—étouffées, gumbos, stuffings—that started in the kitchens of nineteenth-century home cooks whose families came to New Orleans and south Louisiana from France, Spain, Africa, and the Caribbean. With the influence of Native Americans and a wealth of resources, the melting pot created a new style of cooking, one that is different from any other in the United States or the countries that influenced it. The basis of New Orleans tourism, it is the reason why people come to the city again, again, and again. "We come here to eat," they say.

I grew up in Memphis but was lucky enough to have a grandmother who lived on the edge of New Orleans. Every summer my mother and I spent several weeks with her and sometimes a few days between Christmas and New Year's, too. During that time, New Orleans became the Paris of my universe, the center of my fantasies.

When I went home, my friends heard how I'd eaten piles of boiled crabs, cracked their claws, and sucked their meat and about fishermen who donned hip boots, walked into the swamp and scooped up crawfish, which were delicious bugs that we ate. When I was older, I told them how a boyfriend and I made a wrong turn and found ourselves in the middle of a Zulu parade.

My friends had trouble envisioning these escapades, but the tales were so vivid that my best friend's father named me "Good Hope" after the little town where my grandmother lived. I was always going to Good Hope or had been to Good Hope and shared my treasure chest of thrills with all who would listen. Even when I was an adult, he still called me Good Hope.

You can imagine my delight when my engineer husband graduated from Georgia Tech and was offered two jobs in New Orleans. YES! I knew all about New Orleans and especially the food. There were oysters and soft-shell crabs and Beulah Ledner's bakery for the best éclairs and cream puffs in the world. We could go to Middendorf's and eat mountains of crabs, and late-night beignets were just waiting for us at Café Du Monde. I hadn't meant to upset him so, but when we were driving near the lakefront looking for an apartment, I spotted a sign that said "Boiled Crabs" and insisted on having lunch there. He watched me pull off the crabs' legs, clean off the dead man's fingers, pick out the meat, and slather the fat on crackers. I remember his exact words. "You must be a terrible person to eat that," he said. I tried a little more sophistication with my eating frenzies after that but soon reverted to paganism when he, too, discovered the gourmet treat of prying open a fat crab and devouring the succulent meat with its yellow fat as the sauce.

It was a starting point but little did I know what was to come. Before long, I met a friend under the clock at Holmes' and was introduced to the joys of oysters Rockefeller and stuffed eggplant at Galatoire's. I began collecting recipes at dinner parties and saving recipes that NOPSI (New Orleans Public Service, Inc.) circulated on streetcars. I made my own gumbo and entertained with grillades and grits soufflé. I was in heaven.

There was something about New Orleans that inspired me to cook. I would eat an oyster and artichoke soup in a restaurant and want to duplicate it at home. This was during a time when young people had dinner parties and feverishly swapped recipes. Sadly, young people today are so busy with multi-tasking that takeout is all too tempting. Yet the great cooks who sired this food were busy too, washing on scrub boards while red beans simmered, growing their own peppers and tomatoes, and salvaging every leftover morsel for the next day's étouffée and bread pudding.

For those of us who enjoy cooking, it is fun and actually relaxing after a long day at work. Smelling the onions sautéing while sipping a glass of wine and overseeing the homework at the breakfast bar can be a great pleasure. And family time around the dinner table is matchless.

In my mind, there are no better recipes than those handed down to us in south Louisiana. We have a legacy to perpetuate. We have home cooks to thank for their uses of roux, seasonings, sauces, spices, and indigenous ingredients from our waters and soil.

So I say to the young folks. Start your own recipe files. A child in your household may thank you some day. Meanwhile, don't forget to smell the onions.

New
Orleans
HOME COOKING

CHAPTER ONE

Appetizers

Fried Eggplant Fingers

This is a great starter. Just be sure not to eat too many or you'll never make it through the entrée.

1 medium eggplant	2 tbsp. milk
1 cup flour	1 cup breadcrumbs, seasoned
Salt, pepper, and Creole seasoning	Olive or vegetable oil or a
1 egg	combination

Peel eggplant and cut into 4-by-½-inch fingers. Place eggplant pieces on a plate, sprinkle with salt, and cover with another plate. Let eggplant sweat for about 30 minutes, draining the plate several times. Drain a final time and place eggplant pieces on paper towels.

Set out three small flat bowls. Place flour in one and mix in seasonings. Place egg and milk in one and breadcrumbs in the other. With a whisk or fork, beat the egg with milk.

Heat a couple of tablespoons of oil in a large skillet. When medium hot, begin breading the eggplant. First, roll eggplant sticks in the flour and then dip on all sides in the egg wash. Finally, roll eggplant sticks in the breadcrumbs. Place eggplant in the skillet in a single layer and turn as each side browns in order to brown all sides. You may have to reduce heat if eggplant is browning too fast. Take up on paper towels.

The eggplant will soak up the oil quickly so you will have to add a little oil for subsequent batches. Do not overcrowd the skillet.

These are good by themselves or with a marinara dipping sauce that you make yourself or buy in a jar.

Serves 10 as hors d'oeuvres.

Marinated Crabs

This marinated crabs recipe is a takeoff from the famous dish formerly served at Mosca's. The last time I was at the restaurant, the waitress said the dish was taken off the menu because of a lack of requests for it. I could not hide my disappointment because my mouth was set for marinated crabs. Fortunately, we've always made our own at home after a crab boil or just with a few leftover from the seafood store.

1 dozen boiled crabs, well seasoned
1 cup extra-virgin olive oil
2 cups chopped onion
1 cup chopped celery
12 cloves garlic, unpeeled and flattened with the back of a large knife
2 tbsp. chopped parsley

¾ cup white wine vinegar
Juice of 1 lemon
Salt to taste
Pinch cayenne pepper
3 bay leaves, torn
2 tbsp. Italian seasoning
10 turns on a peppermill
1 pint jar olive salad, good quality

Buy crabs freshly boiled from a reputable seafood store. Pull off the backs; scrape off the lungs and everything from the cavity of the crab except the fat. Cut off the eyes. Discard everything but the body, legs, and claws. Cut the crab in half with a sharp knife or kitchen shears. Cut off the claws. Do not pull them, or the meat will pull out of the body. Leave small legs on. With a nutcracker, crack both segments of each claw but try to leave them intact. With a sharp knife, cut off the small piece of shell that holds the lump crabmeat in place. Repeat gently with each crab, placing them in a large bowl.

In a medium bowl, mix well all other ingredients except olive salad. Pour over the crabs and stir very gently to coat all without breaking them up. Tightly seal the top of the bowl with a cover or aluminum foil and place in the refrigerator for at least 8 hours or up to 24. Stir gently several times. An hour before serving, add olive salad and stir gently. Serve in bowls with some of the liquid and plenty of French bread.

Serves 4 as an entrée, 8 as appetizers.

Crab-stuffed Mushrooms

Appetizers come and go, but some are here to stay. That is certainly the case with crab-stuffed mushrooms. What two ingredients go together any better than crabmeat and mushrooms? And, if you don't use too much butter, they are amazingly healthful and low-cal.

1 lb. whole mushrooms (about 30)	2 cloves garlic, minced
1 lb. back fin lump crabmeat	1 tbsp. chopped flat-leafed parsley
3 tbsp. butter, divided	¼ cup breadcrumbs, seasoned
3 tsp. lemon juice, divided	Salt and pepper to taste
3 green onions, minced	¼ cup grated Parmesan cheese

Wipe mushrooms with a damp paper towel to clean them. Remove the stems and reserve for another use. Pick through the crabmeat, removing any shell.

Melt 1½ tbsp. butter in a skillet and add 1½ tsp. lemon juice. Dip each mushroom cap into the butter mixture and place in a 10-by-13-inch baking dish. If there is any left in the skillet, pour it around mushrooms in baking dish. Melt remaining 1½ tbsp. butter and sauté onion and garlic over medium heat for about 2 minutes, stirring. Add parsley, breadcrumbs, salt and pepper, and remaining 1½ tsp. lemon juice. Then gently add the crabmeat, being careful not to break it up too much. Stuff mixture into mushroom caps, mounding them over the top with a spoon and your hand. When they are all stuffed and back in the baking pan, sprinkle them lightly with grated cheese. Bake in a preheated 350-degree oven for about 20 to 30 minutes. If they are not slightly browned on top, run them under the broiler for 1 or 2 minutes. Serve hot.

Serves 10.

Belgian Endive with Crab Salad

Belgian endive makes a spectacular presentation as an hors d'oeuvre. It is also quick and easy with a dollop of something tasty at its stem. Mixed with cream cheese and seasonings, crabmeat makes a perfect stuffing.

2 heads Belgian endive
4 oz. cream cheese
2 tbsp. mayonnaise
2 green onions, minced
1 tbsp. minced flat-leaf parsley
1 tsp. lemon zest

Dash of Worcestershire sauce
Dash of Tabasco
Salt and freshly ground black pepper to taste
½ tsp. Creole seasoning
½ lb. crabmeat, tail or lump

Pull Belgian endive leaves apart, rinse, and pat dry. Mix well all other ingredients except crabmeat. Add crabmeat and toss gently. Spoon 1 tbsp. crab salad onto the stem end of each endive leaf. Arrange stuffed leaves in a circular pattern around a plate or platter.

Makes about 30 hors d'oeuvres.

Hot Crab Dip

Nothing tastes quite as good at a party as hot crab dip. Wherever you place it, the crowds will congregate until the last smidgeon is eaten. It's not hard to make but can be expensive, depending on the cost of crabmeat, which fluctuates with the seasons. The most important step is getting all of the shell out of the crabmeat, which can be purchased by the pound at seafood stores and supermarkets. Jumbo lump, the most expensive, usually has less shell and is easier to pick through. Try to remove shell without breaking up the crabmeat. You want nice chunks of crab throughout the dip. When serving, use a chafing dish and keep the fire low so the dip will not curdle.

2 lb. crabmeat
1 stick butter
1 medium onion, minced or grated
3 green onions, minced
3 cloves garlic, minced
2 8-oz. packages cream cheese, softened

Worcestershire sauce to taste, about 2 tsp.
Tabasco to taste, about 1 tsp.
Creole seasoning to taste, about 2 tsp.
Mayonnaise, about 2 tbsp.

Pick over crabmeat to remove any shells, being careful not to break up crabmeat too much.

In a large skillet, melt butter and sauté onion, green onions, and garlic until soft. Remove from heat. Add remaining ingredients except crabmeat and mix well, adjusting the mayonnaise to reach desired consistency. Gently stir in the crabmeat, again being careful not to break up too much. Place in a chafing dish over low flame and serve with toasts or crackers of choice.

Serves a crowd.

Oysters Bienville

Baked on the half shell, this delectable version of the oyster was named for the founder of New Orleans, Jean Baptiste le Moyne, Sieur de Bienville, and the namesake street on which Arnaud's restaurant is located in the French Quarter. It was invented at the ninety-year-old restaurant supposedly by its founder, Leon Bertrand Arnaud Cazenave, also known as Count Arnaud. It is rich with egg yolks and cream and even incorporates shrimp and mushrooms in its long list of ingredients. Here is a somewhat simpler version sans shrimp and egg yolks.

2 dozen oysters, shucked
½ stick butter
1 bunch green onions, chopped
4 oz. mushrooms, chopped
2 cloves garlic, minced
2 tbsp. flour
1 cup heavy cream

½ cup dry white wine
2 tbsp. sherry
2 tbsp. minced parsley
Salt and freshly ground black
    pepper to taste
¼ tsp. cayenne pepper
¼ cup grated Romano cheese

Drain the oysters, clean the deep half of shells, one for each oyster, and set aside.

Melt butter in a heavy skillet and sauté the green onions, mushrooms, and garlic for about 5 minutes over medium heat. Add flour and cook for 1 minute, stirring. Add cream slowly, stirring, and simmer until thickened. Add all other ingredients and simmer over low heat for several minutes. Cool and then refrigerate until cold.

Preheat oven to 400 degrees. Just before serving time, place oysters in dry shells and place in a large roasting pan lined with rock salt, or in individual aluminum pans lined with rock salt. Top each oyster with a heaping spoonful of the mixture. Bake for about 15 minutes or until browned on top. Serve with hot French bread and lemon wedges.

Serves 2 to 4.

Oysters Rockefeller

French-inspired spirits are part of the mystique of New Orleans. Herbsaint, Sazerac rye whiskey, and Peychaud Bitters go back to the early twentieth century when they were created in New Orleans. Today the three are distilled at the Buffalo Trace Distillery in Franklin County, Kentucky, a company owned by the historic Sazerac Company of New Orleans.

Spirits are not all just for drinking. Leave it to local cooks to tuck them into recipes. Take Herbsaint, a substitute for the illegal absinthe. It is the distinguishing anise taste in oysters Rockefeller, the legendary dish created at Antoine's.

Herbsaint (erb-sant) was first made after Prohibition in the attic of the Uptown home of J. Marion Legendre. It is a greenish-amber liqueur that when mixed with ice or water becomes an opaque gyrating beverage. It contains no poisonous wormwood as did its predecessor, absinthe. The romantic name, herbe sainte in French or royal herb, was chosen by Chef Susan Spicer as the name for her restaurant on St. Charles Avenue.

Huitres en coquille à la Rockefeller was first served at Antoine's in 1899 by Jules Alciatore. A shortage of snails from Europe required a replacement and oysters were just the answer. It was named after John D. Rockefeller because of its "rich" texture. This recipe differs from the original in that it contains spinach. The original is a secret recipe containing a number of green vegetables other than spinach; however, most recipes have added spinach with great success.

3 dozen oysters

1 10-oz. package chopped spinach, thawed and pressed dry

1 stick butter

1 bunch green onions, chopped, green and white parts divided

3 stalks celery with tops, chopped with tops divided

½ bell pepper, chopped

2 cloves garlic, minced

10 large leaves fresh basil, chopped

½ bunch parsley, leaves only, chopped

⅓ cup Herbsaint

Salt and freshly ground pepper to taste

Several shakes Tabasco

Several shakes Worcestershire sauce

⅓ cup breadcrumbs, seasoned

Drain oysters well, reserving liquid for another use such as freezing to use in gumbo. If you are opening live oysters, scrape the oysters off the shells, drain, clean off the flat shell and reserve, and discard the other shell. If buying oysters already shucked, you can place them in a casserole dish and top with Rockefeller sauce, or use clamshells that can be purchased in kitchen stores. Keep oysters and fresh shells refrigerated until time to bake.

Meanwhile, thaw spinach and mash it dry in a colander or large strainer.

In a large skillet or pot, melt the butter and sauté the white part of onions, celery, and bell pepper until limp. Add garlic, green onion tops, and celery tops and sauté for 1 minute. Add spinach, basil, and parsley and sauté 1 minute more. Add Herbsaint, salt, pepper, Tabasco, and Worcestershire and simmer for about 5 minutes. Remove from heat. In a blender, purée half of the mixture until coarsely puréed. Empty into a bowl and coarsely purée the other half. Place in bowl and add breadcrumbs.

If using oysters on the half-shells, place a drained oyster on each shell. Mound the sauce over the oysters on the half-shells, or place oysters in a casserole dish and top with Rockefeller sauce. Sprinkle lightly with a little more breadcrumbs and bake in a preheated 400-degree oven for 15 minutes. If oysters are not browning on top, place under the broiler for a minute or two.

Serves 3 or 4 as an entrée, 6 as appetizers.

Note: This is an easy dish to serve as party food. Bake according to above instructions in a decorative bake-proof dish and serve with bagel chips.

Chargrilled Oysters

It was just over a decade ago that the charbroiled oyster made its debut at Drago's Seafood Restaurant and Oyster Bar in Metairie. Owners Drago and Klara Cvitanovich had a long attachment to oysters, being immigrants from Croatia where the oyster industry serves much of Europe. Croatian oystermen migrated to Louisiana two centuries ago and still dominate the local industry today. Having worked at his brother-in-law's restaurant in Lakeview, also named Drago's, Cvitanovich opened his own in 1970, buying oysters from Croatian friends in the business. However, their son, Tommy Cvitanovich, now owner-manager, is the one responsible for the signature dish of the three hundred-seat restaurant. "I had the idea about fourteen or fifteen years ago," said the namesake for Drumfish Tommy. The sauce on that dish was so good that he wanted to try it on the oysters. He added two cheeses, Parmesan and Romano, and a star was born. On a good day, he said, the restaurant serves more than nine hundred dozen charbroiled oysters.

The good news for home cooks is that charbroiled oysters are easy to prepare in your own back yard.

"Buy the freshest you can buy," says Tommy Cvitanovich. "And get big ones." A real time saver is using the kind of aluminum shells that are used to stuff crabs. Just cut the tips off the shells and put two oysters in each shell, he said.

Then, cook them as fast as you can. "The hotter the fire, the better," he said. At Drago's, cooks spray water onto the roaring fire to create steam. Most importantly, serve them and eat them immediately. "We try to have them hit the table sizzling," Cvitanovich said.

Chargrilled oysters are great to serve at an outdoor or patio party. Guests love to watch them cook. The only problem is that oysters generally are sold by the sack or half sack from a seafood dealer. Therefore, somebody in your group needs to know how to shuck them. Look at it this way. Shucking them is half the fun. Just get a couple of oyster knives, some heavy gloves, and two people who know what they're doing.

4 dozen oysters
2 sticks butter
2 cloves garlic, crushed
Juice of 1 lemon
1 tbsp. Worcestershire sauce

½ tsp. Tabasco
Black pepper to taste
Parmesan cheese, about 1 cup,
    grated

Shuck oysters, cutting each loose from its shell. Place oyster in one shell and discard the other. Choose the deepest shell if it sits straight, or the one that sits the straightest. Reserve some of the oyster water in the shell that you are using.

In a saucepan, melt butter and sauté garlic briefly. Add lemon juice, Worcestershire sauce, Tabasco, and pepper and stir together.

Light a charcoal fire to its hottest temperature, or, a gas grill can be used. Place a dozen oysters in their shells on the grill and immediately spoon 1 tbsp. of sauce mixture over each oyster. Sprinkle each oyster with a thin coating of Parmesan cheese. Close the grill and cook for several minutes until oysters curl. Serve immediately with cocktail forks. Repeat. If grill is large, several dozen can be done at one time.

Serves 4.

Note: Chargrilled oysters are great to pass as a hors d'oeuvre as they come off the grill.

Shrimp Rémoulade

W hat makes shrimp rémoulade so appealing to the cook is that it can be served as hors d'oeuvres or as a first course at the table. To pass before dinner, simply place the rémoulade sauce in a bowl in the center of a platter with the boiled shrimp and toothpicks all around it. If serving at the table, mound shrimp over a bed of shredded lettuce and splash the rémoulade on top.

I bag crab boil
Salt and cayenne pepper to taste
I lemon, cut into wedges
2 lb. large shrimp
4 tbsp. ketchup
I tbsp. fresh horseradish
½ cup Creole mustard
I tbsp. lemon juice
I tbsp. Worcestershire sauce

I tbsp. Tabasco
¼ cup white wine vinegar
½ cup virgin or extra-virgin olive oil
I rib celery, chopped
2 tbsp. minced parsley
3 green onions, chopped
Lettuce, shredded

Bring a large pot of water to a boil. Add crab boil, salt, cayenne, and lemon wedges. When the water comes to a boil, add shrimp. Bring back to a boil, boil for 1 minute, turn off heat, and let shrimp soak for 10 minutes. Drain.

To make rémoulade sauce, mix in a blender the ketchup, horseradish, Creole mustard, lemon juice, Worcestershire, Tabasco, and vinegar. Add the olive oil gradually. Add salt and cayenne pepper to taste. Add the celery, parsley, and green onions and blend for about 2 seconds, leaving some small pieces. This sauce can be made a day or two in advance.

When ready to serve, place a bed of lettuce on each plate. Top with peeled, deveined shrimp. Cover shrimp with sauce. This is best served very cold.

Or, serve rémoulade sauce in a bowl, centered on a platter of shrimp. If peeling shrimp, leave tails on for easy serving. Or, serve with toothpicks.

Serves 6 as appetizers or hors d'oeuvres.

Shrimp Wrapped in Bacon

Long ago, I discovered a real barbecued shrimp recipe that never fails to wow a crowd. I say "real" because what many of us call barbecued shrimp is actually cooked in the oven. This one cooks on the outdoor grill. You simply wrap large shrimp in pieces of bacon and grill them over a charcoal fire. Using a hickory-smoked bacon gives all the flavor you could want with no other seasoning necessary. These make great dippers in a cocktail sauce to serve as an appetizer on the patio. Except for peeling and deveining the shrimp, the recipe is simple. The larger the shrimp, the easier and quicker the preparation.

2 lb. large shrimp   **Toothpicks**
1 lb. bacon

Peel and devein shrimp. Cut bacon into thirds so that each piece is about 3 inches long. Wrap each shrimp in a piece of bacon. Fasten with 2 toothpicks.

Heat a charcoal or gas grill to hot. Place grill about 6 to 8 inches above coals. Place shrimp on grill and cook until bacon is browning on one side. Turn shrimp to brown bacon on all sides. When bacon is done, shrimp will be done. Serve with cocktail sauce for dipping.

Note: Stainless steel skewers can be used instead of toothpicks. Thread 4 to 6 bacon-wrapped shrimp onto skewer and grill, turning as bacon browns. To serve as a first course, remove shrimp from skewers and serve on small plates with individual dipping sauces.

Dipping sauce: Combine $3/4$ cup ketchup with 1 tbsp. Worcestershire sauce, 1 tbsp. horseradish, 1 tsp. lemon juice, and $1/2$ tsp. Tabasco.

Serves 6 as hors d'oeuvres or first course.

Crawfish-stuffed Bread

My daughter Jennifer had to go to Jazz Fest every year if for no other reason than to get the crawfish-stuffed bread. Finally, she learned to make it herself and found it a great dish to serve at a party. Learning to cook some of the fine specialties served at the festival means you can have your own Jazz Fest at home. Put on some Aaron Neville or Irma Thomas and you're rockin' and rollin' whenever you please.

PASTRY:
1 package active dry yeast
2 tbsp. vegetable oil
1 tbsp. sugar
1 ¼ cups warm water
3 ½ cups all-purpose flour
1 tsp. salt

FILLING:
6 oz. Monterey Jack cheese, grated
6 oz. extra-sharp cheddar cheese, grated

2 tsp. vegetable oil
⅓ cup chopped onions
⅓ cup chopped green onions, green part only
1 12-oz. package crawfish tails, thawed
½ tsp. garlic powder
¼ tsp. cayenne pepper
½ tsp. salt
Freshly ground black pepper to taste
1 egg white, beaten

In the bowl of an electric mixer, whisk together the yeast, oil, sugar, and warm water until well mixed. Let it sit for a few minutes until slightly foamy. Attach dough hook to mixer and add flour gradually and salt, kneading on low speed until the dough begins to cling together. Increase speed slightly until dough forms a ball. Remove dough from mixer and place on a floured board. With your hands, make the ball smooth and round. Grease your hands with a little vegetable oil and pat the dough on all sides. Place in a large bowl, cover with plastic wrap and let it rise to almost double in size.

While the dough is rising, grate and mix cheeses and set aside.

In the vegetable oil, sauté the white onions until translucent, add the green onion tops and sauté a minute more. Add crawfish and seasonings and simmer, covered, for 10 minutes. Set aside to cool.

When dough has risen, place on floured board and cut into half. Roll out ½ to $\frac{1}{8}$ inch thin and cut into 6 rectangular pieces. Place 2 tbsp. of cheese on one side of each dough piece, leaving a $\frac{1}{2}$-inch margin, and place 2 tbsp. of crawfish mixture on top of cheese. Brush edges of dough with beaten egg white and fold over to make a square or rectangle. Pinch edges together. Place on a baking pan covered with parchment paper. Repeat with other half of dough until all pastries are complete. You should have 12 small loaves. Brush tops with egg white and cut 2 slits in the tops of each. Cover loosely with plastic wrap, and let rise again for about 1 hour.

Preheat oven to 400 degrees. Bake for about 30 minutes or until loaves are golden brown.

Makes 12 loaves.

Sausage Balls

Casual gatherings such as football parties demand lots of simple food that can be picked up and eaten without fuss. Toothpick food such as sausage balls require little effort to eat or cook. Make them a day ahead of time, and heat them up when ready to serve.

5 green onions, minced
2 cloves garlic, minced
2 lb. Italian sausage
1 egg, beaten

$\frac{1}{2}$ cup Italian breadcrumbs
Salt, pepper, and cayenne to taste
$\frac{1}{4}$ cup grated Parmesan cheese
1 jar hot pepper jelly

Finely mince onions and garlic. Remove sausage from casings, if necessary. In a large bowl, mix onions and garlic with sausage. Add remaining ingredients, except pepper jelly, and mix well. Roll into 1-inch balls and place on a baking sheet. Bake in a preheated 400-degree oven until brown, about 20 minutes, stirring frequently. When ready to serve, heat jar of pepper jelly in the microwave. Add a tablespoon or two of water to thin to dipping consistency. Serve on toothpicks with melted hot pepper jelly for dipping.

Serves 15 to 20 as hors d'oeuvres.

Daube Glacé

If ever there were a classic for the south Louisiana Christmas season, it is the daube glacé, a spicy mold of jellied meat. Much like hogshead cheese—except that the meat of choice is beef—it is served in thin slices on toast points, garlic croutons, or crackers. A perfect hors d'oeuvre, it was a favorite of the early Creoles as an elegant way to utilize a small amount of meat, even leftovers. In fact, a beef daube can be served as one meal with leftovers and plenty of additional spices providing the follow-up glacé.

The Creoles also called the dish daube froide à la Creole, or cold meat that has been braised in stock and wine with herbs. A touch of pork, usually pigs' feet, gives the finished dish its gelled consistency although some modern recipes leave them out in favor of dry gelatin.

Old cookbooks mention daube glacé being served traditionally in New Orleans on holidays and specifically at weddings in Cajun country. At lunch, it was often served as an entrée with salad and croutons, but by popular demand, it has evolved as an appetizer for holiday parties or wedding receptions.

The easy part is that it can be made ahead of time and kept for several days. It is best to make the recipe over a period of two days, cooking the daube one day and putting the molds together the next. Pouring it into fancy smaller molds means you can give it as gifts, take it to parties, or use it to entertain on several occasions. If the molds are very small, you will have to chop the meat into smaller pieces.

1 3-lb. beef roast, such as rump or shoulder

3 cloves garlic, peeled and cut into slivers

Salt, pepper, and Creole seasoning (about ½ tsp. each)

2 tbsp. vegetable oil

4 10½-oz. cans condensed beef consommé with gelatin, plus equal amount of water

½ cup madeira

1 large onion, sliced

3 carrots, cut into chunks

2 turnips, sliced

2 lb. pigs' feet

2 bay leaves

Several sprigs thyme

Salt and pepper, about ¼ tsp. each

1 tbsp. cayenne pepper

1 envelope gelatin

8 thin lemon slices

Flat-leaf parsley

Olives with pimento stuffing, sliced

Cut narrow, deep slits in roast and stuff slits with slivers of garlic. Sprinkle ½ tsp. each salt, pepper, and Creole seasoning all over roast. Heat oil in a large heavy pot or Dutch oven and brown roast on all sides. When browned well, add consommé, madeira, onion, carrots, and turnips, cover and simmer for 4 hours, until the meat is falling apart.

While roast is cooking, simmer pigs' feet in water to cover in a separate smaller pot with bay leaves, 3 sprigs of thyme, remaining salt and pepper, and cayenne pepper, covered, for about 2 hours.

When all meats are cooked and tender, strain stocks into a large bowl or pot and stir in gelatin until well blended. If stock has cooled, heat a little in a bowl and stir in gelatin until it is dissolved. Add it back to stock.

Spray 3 loaf pans, preferably glass, or one large terrine, or several smaller terrines or molds with non-stick spray. When stock has cooled, pour just enough into each mold to measure ¼ inch. Decorate what will become the tops of the molds with thin lemon slices, sprigs of thyme, parsley leaves, and thin slices of pimento-stuffed olives. Place in the refrigerator to set. This should take at least an hour.

Meanwhile, pull roast into shreds and/or chop into cubes. A combination of shreds and cubes is good. Pick meat from pigs' feet and discard the rest. Add the small amount of pork to the beef. Optionally, some of the carrot can be sliced or chopped and added for color.

When topping is set, divide meat equally and place in molds. Skim fat from stock and pour cooled stock into molds within $1/2$ inch of the top. Save any leftover stock for another use. Cover with plastic wrap and place in refrigerator for 10 to 12 hours until firmly set. Skim off any fat that accumulates on top. This can be made ahead and held for several days in the refrigerator.

When ready to serve, run a sharp knife around edges of molds and set molds in 1 inch of hot water for a few seconds. Place serving platter over each mold and invert. Decorate platter with more parsley or greens and lemon slices and serve with French bread toasts, garlic croutons, or crackers. You can slice mold into thin pieces or let guests slice it themselves.

Note: Another way to make the molds and serve the glacé is to use 9-by-13-inch glass baking dishes. Then the molds can be sliced into small squares with slices placed on serving dishes. For the above recipe, I used one glass loaf pan, one 7-by-11-inch baking dish, and one medium bowl. I served the molds whole on platters to let guests slice their own, and I cut thin squares from the baking dish and placed them on a plate with crackers on the side.

Natchitoches Meat Pies

The town of Natchitoches is known for its meat pies. Many cultures have their meat pies, and Louisiana's are believed to have originated with the Natchitoches Indians. They are much like Spanish empanadas. They are a hot item at Jazz Fest, and many chefs around the state create their own versions.

FILLING:
- I lb. lean ground beef, such as ground round
- I lb. lean ground pork
- 2 tbsp. vegetable oil
- 2 tbsp. flour
- I onion, chopped
- 4 green onions, chopped
- 2 cloves garlic, minced
- I tsp. salt
- ½ tsp. Creole seasoning
- ¾ tsp. cayenne pepper
- Freshly ground black pepper
- I tbsp. chopped parsley

CRUST:
- 3 tbsp. shortening
- 2 eggs
- 6 tbsp. milk
- 2½ cups flour plus extra for rolling
- I egg white, beaten

To make filling: In a skillet, brown beef and pork, breaking the meat up well. Set aside.

In a medium pot, make a peanut butter-colored roux with the oil and flour. Add onions, stirring for several minutes, and then garlic, stirring for another minute. Remove from heat and add meat and remaining ingredients. Mix well and set aside.

To make crust: Flour a large cutting board. In a mixer, cream shortening. Add eggs one at a time, mix, and blend in milk. Add flour and mix on high until just blended. Mixture should cling together. Place on floured board and form into a smooth ball. Do not overhandle the dough or it will become tough. Place in a large Ziploc bag and refrigerate for at least 30 minutes.

When ready to fry the pies, heat enough oil to cover 2 or 3 at a time, or use a deep fryer, heating oil to 350 degrees.

On the floured board, cut the ball of dough into six equal pieces. Roll out one piece at a time the size of a saucer, 6 or 7 inches round and about $\frac{1}{8}$ inch thick. An easy way to do this is to place the saucer down on the rolled-out dough and cut the pastry with a knife.

Use scraps for 1 or 2 more.

To form the pastries: Place $\frac{1}{3}$ cup of the filling on one side of the pastry circle, leaving $\frac{1}{2}$-inch rim. With your finger, brush the egg white around the entire $\frac{1}{2}$-inch rim of the pastry. Fold over and press the edges together with a fork.

Drop pastries, 2 or 3 at a time, into hot oil and fry, turning occasionally, until golden brown, about 5 minutes. Drain on paper towels and continue frying until all are done. Serve hot.

Makes 6 to 8.

Note: You will have filling left over. Either freeze it for another time, or make another round of pastry to use immediately.

CHAPTER TWO

Soups

Seafood Gumbo

In the city, seafood gumbo reigns supreme. Go to the country and you'll find chicken and sausage gumbo. Some people mix it all up, including smoked turkey necks. I am a purist for the sweet finesse of fresh (raw) crabs, shrimp, and oysters in seafood gumbo. The rest of my family prefers the chicken kind. Ask many a New Orleanian and they'll say they like the turkey gumbo after Thanksgiving. I'll go for that, too, but I have to add oysters. For thickening, some add okra during the cooking while others add filé powder (sassafras leaves) to individual bowls when serving. City folks add tomato; Cajuns keep it brown. My, this must be confusing to people who don't live in south Louisiana. One thing for sure: All gumbo begins with a roux. (Well, even that is debatable.) Most cooks use a recipe passed down from one generation to the next. Here is my favorite, but please see other versions in the cookbook.

1 ½ lb. shrimp, peeled and deveined, shells reserved
½ lb. fresh okra
½ cup vegetable oil
½ cup flour
1 large onion, chopped
1 bell pepper, chopped
2 stalks celery, chopped
1 bunch green onions, chopped, green and white parts divided
3 cloves garlic, minced
⅓ cup andouille, chopped

1 16-oz. can tomatoes, or 2 large fresh Creole tomatoes in season, peeled and chopped
1 package gumbo crabs, or 4 to 6 small crabs, uncooked and cleaned
1 pint oysters with their liquor
2 bay leaves
Salt, cayenne pepper, and Creole seasoning to taste
1 tsp. thyme leaves
2 tbsp. chopped parsley

Set shrimp aside in the refrigerator and place heads and shells in a pot and cover with water. Simmer, covered, for 30 minutes to make stock. Strain and reserve.

Chop okra into $1/4$ inch rounds and cook, stirring, in a skillet coated in cooking spray until liquid evaporates and stickiness dries up. Set aside.

In a large, heavy pot, make a dark brown roux from oil and flour. Add onion, bell pepper, celery, and white parts of onions and sauté until soft. Add garlic and andouille and sauté a few more minutes. Add tomato and cook a little longer. Add crabs, liquor strained from oysters, and shrimp stock to equal about 6 cups of liquid and seasonings. Simmer, covered, for 45 minutes.

Add shrimp and continue simmering for 10 minutes. Add green onion tops and oysters and cook until oysters curl, about 5 minutes. Remove from fire and add parsley. Serve over rice.

Serves 6 to 8.

Louisiana Bouillabaisse

A Louisiana bouillabaisse is simply a classic bouillabaisse using Louisiana seafood. Of course, you can add lobster, mussels, and clams as you wish, but for practical purposes, this recipe relies on the highly available local ingredients. One of the great seafood soups in the world, bouillabaisse is a dish of fish and shellfish with herbs and is associated with the Provence region of France, particularly Marseille. It was originally cooked on the beach by fishermen. There are many arguments about how to make it and what types of fish should be used. It began with whatever was available. Fishermen added the rouille as an accompaniment to the soup. It can be sprinkled on the soup or just spread on toasted French bread croutons, which are a must for serving with the bouillabaisse.

2 lb. whole red snapper, grouper,
   or amberjack (or 1 lb. fillets)
1 lb. shrimp
1 dozen oysters and their liquor
2 onions, chopped, divided
2 leeks, chopped
2 stalks celery, chopped
3 cloves garlic, minced, divided
Freshly ground black pepper
2 bay leaves
2 tbsp. extra-virgin olive oil

1 fennel bulb, chopped
3 medium ripe tomatoes, peeled,
   seeded, and chopped
Leaves from 4 sprigs of thyme
1 cup dry white wine
Pinch saffron
2 tbsp. chopped flat-leaf parsley
Salt and freshly ground black
   pepper to taste
1 lb. uncooked crabs, such as
   gumbo crabs

If buying whole fish, fillet it, saving the head and bones. Peel shrimp, saving the heads and peelings. Drain the oysters, saving their liquor.

In a stockpot, place the head and bones of the fish, shrimp heads and peelings, oyster liquor, 1 onion, leeks, celery, 1 garlic clove, pepper, and bay leaves and cover with water. Bring to a boil, lower heat, and simmer for 30 minutes. Drain and reserve stock.

In a heavy pot, sauté in oil remaining onion, 2 garlic cloves, and fennel until soft. Add the reserved stock, plus enough water to make 6 cups, tomatoes, thyme, wine, saffron, parsley, salt, and pepper, and simmer for 15 minutes. Add crabs and simmer 5 minutes more. Cut fish fillets into 2-inch chunks. Add these and shrimp to soup and cook for 3 minutes. Add oysters and cook until they curl. Remove from heat, taste and adjust seasonings. When ready to serve, heat and serve in large bowls with French bread croutons and rouille.

To make the rouille: Cook 2 egg yolks with 2 tbsp. of the bouillabaisse liquid over very low heat, stirring constantly, until the mixture coats a metal spoon with a thin film, bubbles at the edges, or reaches 160 degrees. Immediately place the saucepan in ice water and stir until the yolk mixture is cool. (Traditionally, raw eggs are used; heating is a safeguard against the rare salmonella.) Place in a blender the egg yolk mixture, 4 cloves peeled garlic, 2 hot red peppers such as cayenne, 2 slices of bread torn in pieces, and $\frac{1}{2}$ tsp. salt. Blend and then slowly add $\frac{1}{2}$ cup extra-virgin olive oil until the mixture had emulsified and thickened. Serve this to spread on croutons with bouillabaisse.

To make the French bread croutons: Slice as much as you want of a po-boy-size loaf into $\frac{1}{2}$-inch rounds. Slice a clove of garlic into a $\frac{1}{2}$ cup of olive oil and let it sit for 10 minutes. Then rub a little of the oil on each slice of bread. Heat in a 300-degree oven until toasted, about 15 minutes.

Crawfish Bisque

I describe crawfish bisque as the most difficult dish I have ever cooked. And, I have only cooked it twice in my life—from scratch. Be that as it may, the positives might be said to outweigh the negatives. That's because crawfish bisque is the most delicious thing I've ever put in my mouth, and preparing it can be a lot of fun if you make it a party. The good news is that the availability of frozen crawfish tails creates shortcuts that can put this amazing dish on your table in no time at all.

Traditionally, we started with about fifty pounds of live crawfish, killed them quickly in boiling water, peeled all the tails, and saved the shells around the heads. That was the time-consuming part, along with stuffing the shells. By using frozen tails, the dish is no harder than making an étouffée and the "stuffing" can be added meatball-style.

In the river parishes and bayou country a few years back, every good cook had a freezer full of crawfish bisque that took days and weeks to prepare. Hurricane season threatened the loss of the priceless containers when power was lost after a storm. This was especially true before the era of crawfish farming when crawfish were available only from January to June.

As time goes by, crawfish bisque is nearly a lost art of Cajun cooking. However, it doesn't have to be. Just save the outer shells from a crawfish boil and buy your peeled crawfish tails at the store.

If you are among the fearless Louisiana cooks (and there are multitudes) who shuck their own oysters and fry their own turkeys, then by all means start with a fifty-pound sack of live crawfish. Start up the pot with plain water and plunge about half the crawfish at a time into the water for ten minutes only. This kills them and makes them peelable. When cool enough to handle, peel, reserving as much fat as possible. Save the large head shells for stuffing. Depending on how many people are peeling, you may want to do this one day and make the bisque the next.

A word of warning: Do not attempt to peel a fifty-pound sack of crawfish late in the season (after April). I did this once when the crawfish were more mature and their shells harder and thicker and my hands were scarred for a week. Early in the season, the shells are tender and much easier to handle. In addition, having tackled this job on two occasions with only one other person peeling, I recommend involving at least four people.

Another note about making crawfish bisque: A highly important ingredient for the authentic version of bisque is the crawfish fat. There may be a few seafood stores still selling containers of it, but it would be a rare find indeed. Instead, you can buy packages of "crawfish tails and fat." I have stripped the fat from the heads I cleaned for stuffing to divide between the bisque and stuffing. Here is the shortcut version:

3 lb. crawfish tails, preferably
   Louisiana tails with fat
80 crawfish shells (also called
   heads), saved from a crawfish
   boil
2 large onions, divided
2 bell peppers, divided
4 cloves garlic, divided
¾ cup vegetable oil
1 cup flour
1¾ tsp. salt, divided
1½ tsp. cayenne pepper, divided
⅓ cup water

Extra crawfish fat, about ½ cup,
   optional
½ cup breadcrumbs, made in a
   food processor from stale
   French bread
4 tbsp. green onion tops, divided
4 tbsp. parsley, divided
1 tbsp. butter, softened
Flour for coating
6 cups stock and water
1 tbsp. tomato paste
2 bay leaves
¼ tsp. thyme leaves

Divide crawfish tails in half. In a food processor, chop half for bisque, and mince (grind consistency) the other half for the stuffing. Boil cleaned shells in water to cover for 10 minutes to clean. Strain and save water for stock.

Prepare the vegetables in a food processor, chopping 1 onion, 1 bell pepper, and 2 cloves garlic for the bisque and mincing 1 onion, 1 bell pepper, and 2 cloves garlic for the stuffing.

In a heavy pot, make a medium-dark roux (peanut butter colored) with oil and flour. Set aside.

To make the stuffed heads: In a heavy pot, sauté the minced vegetables in $\frac{1}{3}$ cup of the roux. Add the ground tails, about $\frac{3}{4}$ tsp. each salt and cayenne pepper, and about $\frac{1}{3}$ cup of water. If you have extra crawfish fat, add half of it now. Simmer for about 10 minutes. Remove from heat and add breadcrumbs and 2 tbsp. each minced onion tops and parsley. When combined well, add softened butter. Stuff mixture into shells. Roll shells lightly in flour, place on a baking sheet and bake in a preheated 350-degree oven for about 15 minutes. Turn once during baking. Set aside.

To make the bisque, sauté the chopped vegetables in the remainder of the roux. Gradually add 6 cups stock and water if needed, the tomato paste, bay leaves, and thyme and simmer for about 15 minutes. Meanwhile, place half of the remaining crawfish in the food processor and mince. Add this and the chopped crawfish, 1 tsp. salt, and $\frac{3}{4}$ tsp. cayenne pepper and cook 15 more minutes. Add 2 tbsp. each chopped green onion tops and parsley. When ready to serve, add stuffed heads and heat. Serve hot in bowls with rice and about 6 to 8 stuffed heads per serving.

Serves 8.

Oyster-artichoke Soup

Could there be a better combination than oysters and artichokes? Not in my book. It is said to have originated in the kitchen of the late Warren LeRuth, who gifted the Westbank of New Orleans with gourmet dining. The man was so talented that not only is his restaurant legendary, he created recipes for many national restaurants and was known for his development of a phenomenal vanilla flavoring and a divine frozen custard. His oyster-artichoke soup has been copied by almost every chef who has ever cooked in New Orleans and a lot of home cooks, too. Talk about easy. Try the following version for a gourmet meal in less than an hour.

3 dozen oysters and their water
½ stick butter
1 bunch green onions, chopped
2 stalks celery, chopped
2 cloves garlic, minced
1 9-oz. package frozen artichoke
   hearts, thawed and coarsely
   chopped
2 tbsp. flour

2 14.5-oz. cans chicken stock
Salt, if needed, freshly ground
   black pepper, and Creole
   seasoning to taste
Pinch of dried thyme
1 tsp. Worcestershire sauce
Shot of Tabasco
1 cup half-and-half
Chopped parsley, optional

Pick over oysters to remove any shell. Separate them from their water, saving the water.

In a medium-sized heavy pot, melt butter and sauté onions, celery, and garlic until soft. Add artichoke hearts and sauté a minute more. Stir in flour until smooth. Gradually add chicken stock and reserved oyster water, stirring, and then seasonings, Worcestershire, and Tabasco. Do not add salt until after the oysters are added because you may not need any, depending on how salty the oysters are. Lower heat and simmer, covered, for about 30 minutes. Add oysters and simmer for a few minutes until oysters curl. Stir in half-and-half and heat gently when ready to serve. Serve with a little chopped parsley on top of each portion, if desired.

Serves 4.

Turtle Soup

It was hard to describe what people missed most about New Orleans during the evacuation caused by Hurricane Katrina. Of course, it was homes and families at first. But after most people were settled somewhere else, at least for a while, they began to long for chicory coffee, creamy red beans, oyster po-boys, and gumbo. For some, it was a cup of turtle soup at Mandina's or a soft-shell crab the way Deanie's fries them.

You won't run into turtle soup many places, but in New Orleans there are dozens of restaurants that make it. Even a few seafood outlets sell dressed turtle meat so it is possible to make at home. Nothing is better on a cold winter night, especially for a parade party.

Turtle soup and Carnival have special connections in a kind of a behind-the-scenes sort of way. Men's organizations traditionally serve it in their krewe quarters where they dress for the balls. Then, before the courts are seated at the supper dances following the balls, they and their families are frequently treated to cups of turtle soup.

This rich, deeply flavored dish is part of the fabric of New Orleans. If gumbo is the dish that epitomizes our food, then turtle soup is one that makes it unique.

2 lb. turtle meat*
Salt
Freshly ground pepper
1 stick butter, divided
2½ qt. (10 cups) strong beef broth, preferably made from beef or veal bones, or canned
8 tbsp. flour
1 large onion, chopped
1 large bell pepper, chopped
2 large stalks celery, chopped
3 large cloves garlic, minced
2 bay leaves
1 tsp. thyme leaves

½ tsp. allspice
1 tbsp. Creole seasoning
Salt and freshly ground pepper to taste
¼ tsp. cayenne pepper or to taste
2 tbsp. Worcestershire sauce
½ cup dry sherry
2 cups tomatoes, diced, fresh or canned
2 tbsp. lemon juice
2 tbsp. minced flat-leaf parsley
Thin lemon slices
2 eggs, boiled and chopped

Chop thawed turtle meat into small dice. Sprinkle with salt and freshly ground pepper. In a heavy skillet, heat on high 1 tbsp. of the butter and sauté meat, a little at a time, on all sides until well browned. Add about 1 cup of stock to deglaze the skillet and leave on a simmer while completing the next step.

In a large heavy pot, heat remaining butter and add flour to make a roux. Stir constantly over medium-high heat until roux is the color of peanut butter. Add and sauté onions, bell pepper, and celery until soft. Add garlic and continue sautéing until vegetables are caramelized. Add turtle meat and all of the juices and brown bits in the bottom of the skillet. Add remaining broth, bay leaves, thyme leaves, allspice, Creole seasoning, salt, pepper, cayenne pepper, Worcestershire, sherry, tomatoes, and lemon juice and bring almost to a boil. Reduce heat to a simmer, cover and cook for 2 hours, until meat is tender. To obtain desired consistency, you may have to take some or all of the meat and solids out with a slotted spoon and grind roughly in a food processor. When cooking is complete, add parsley.

When ready to serve, garnish with lemon slices and boiled eggs. Offer additional sherry if desired.

Serves 8 to 10.

For crowds at Carnival parties, you can double or triple the recipe and self-serve from heated pots into small disposable hot drink cups. The soup can be made ahead of time and frozen.

*Boneless turtle meat is sold frozen at some seafood stores in 2-lb. containers.

Brie-crab Soup

So many famous recipes have been created in New Orleans. Oysters Rockefeller at Antoine's. Arnaud's oysters Bienville. Bananas Foster at Brennan's. And many more. One of the latest to enter the hall of fame is crabmeat and Brie soup from chef Kim Kringlie of The Dakota Restaurant in Covington. His rich and succulent soup keeps lines forming every year at the New Orleans Wine & Food Experience and is a main draw for diners who cross the twenty-four-mile Causeway to visit his restaurant. I once drove the distance mainly for the soup only to learn that crabs weren't in season and the chef wouldn't think of using frozen ones. For the home cook, here is my version using gumbo crabs that are readily available frozen. You must, however, have the fresh lump crabmeat to add when ready to serve. You can usually find this at seafood outlets, but out of season, the price goes up, up, up.

1 1-lb. package frozen gumbo crabs	3 cups water
8 tbsp. (1 stick) butter, divided	Salt and freshly ground pepper
1 onion, chopped	1/4 tsp. cayenne pepper
2 stalks celery, chopped	1/3 cup flour
2 cloves garlic, chopped	5 oz. brie cheese
2 bay leaves	1 cup heavy cream
1 cup white wine	1/2 lb. lump crabmeat

Thaw and rinse gumbo crabs. In a large pot, melt 2 tbsp. of the butter. Add crabs, onion, celery, garlic, and bay leaves. Sauté over medium-high heat for 10 minutes, stirring occasionally. Add wine, water, 1 tsp. salt, several grinds from a pepper mill, and cayenne. Cover and simmer for 1 hour. When cool enough to handle, strain the stock into a bowl or another pot and discard remaining contents.

Clean original pot and melt remaining 6 tbsp. butter, add flour, and stir over medium heat to make a blonde roux. Take about 1/2 cup of stock and add it to the roux, stirring until thickened. Slowly add rest of stock and stir until well blended. Remove rind from Brie, cut Brie into chunks, and add to pot. Simmer, stirring occasionally, until cheese has melted. Stir in heavy cream and simmer until warm. Add crabmeat and serve.

Serves 8.

Gumbo Z'herbes

Seven greens make a green gumbo, a Lenten favorite that is meatless during Lent but often seasoned with ham or andouille at other times. Legend has it that for every green put into the gumbo, a new friend will be made in that year. The common choices are cabbage, spinach, beet and carrot tops, parsley, green onion, various fresh herbs, and mustard, collard, and turnip greens.

Peculiar to New Orleans and labeled a gumbo, it was created by inventive Creole cooks who combined Native American ingredients, African techniques, and Caribbean flavors. They initially served the soup on Good Friday. If meat was used, veal brisket or lean ham were favored. Oddly enough, okra is not an ingredient of most green gumbos. Nor did early cooks see fit to make a roux. Later recipes used the roux but some cooks preferred filé powder, a thickening agent made from the young and tender leaves of the sassafras. As with all gumbos, every cook has his own way of making it.

1 bunch collard greens
1 bunch mustard greens
1 bunch turnip greens
1 bunch kale
½ cabbage, shredded
1 bunch beet tops
1 bunch carrot tops
½ bunch Italian flat-leaf parsley,
    leaves only
1 bunch watercress
1 bunch (or bag) spinach
1 bunch radish tops
1 bunch green onions, chopped,
    white and green parts separated
3 stalks celery with a lot of the
    leaves, chopped

¾ cup vegetable oil
1 cup flour
1 large onion, chopped
2 cloves garlic, minced
1 lb. andouille sausage, sliced, or
    smoked ham, cut in chunks, or
    a combination of both,
    optional*
Salt, pepper, and Creole seasoning
    to taste, about ½ tsp. each
3 bay leaves
1 tsp. thyme leaves
¼ tsp. marjoram
2 qt. water or vegetable stock

Choose at least seven of the above greens. Rinse well, making sure that no soil, sand, or insects cling to the greens. Remove any coarse or tough ribs. Greens can be cleaned with several rinsings in a sink or leaf-by-leaf under running water. Rough-chop all and set aside.

In a large, heavy pot, make a medium-dark roux with oil and flour. Add chopped white onion and celery stalks and sauté until soft. Add garlic and sauté a minute longer. Add meat, seasonings, half the water or stock, and the greens including the green onion and celery tops, cover and simmer for about 30 minutes, stirring occasionally. Add remaining stock and simmer for 1½ more hours, stirring occasionally. Taste and adjust seasonings. Serve with boiled rice.

Serves 8.

*Traditionally, the gumbo is made with meat except during Lent. When not using meat, seasonings and spices can be increased slightly and might include a clove and sprinkle of allspice.

Vegetable Soup

What I call vegetable soup could actually be called beef soup because big chunks of stew meat dominate the pot. But I am particular about what vegetables go in. I was born lucky enough to grow up eating fresh vegetables from my parents' own garden or from farmers' markets or grocery stores. A canned vegetable to me is something that has to be drained and rinsed to get the taste of the can out. I once saw someone make vegetable soup out of one hundred percent canned vegetables and thought, "Why bother?" The essence of the soup is created as the ingredients cook and break down. Vegetable soup with meat must cook for a while in order to tenderize the cheaper cuts of beef that are commonly used. But there is no need to drop in most vegetables until the meat is tender. I don't like them overcooked. A big pot of vegetable soup makes great leftovers to place in containers for a later meal or to give to a friend just home from the hospital.

1 ½ lb. beef stew meat or beef
  soup bones, trimmed of excess
  fat, or a combination
Creole seasoning to rub
2 tbsp. vegetable oil
1 large onion, chopped
1 bell pepper, chopped
2 stalks celery, chopped
2 cloves garlic, minced
2 medium fresh tomatoes, peeled
  and chopped, or 1 14-oz. can
  plum tomatoes
1 6-oz. can tomato paste
2 14-oz. cans beef broth
4 cups water

½ tsp. salt
¼ tsp. pepper
½ tsp. Creole seasoning
¼ tsp. Italian seasoning
¼ lb. fresh green beans, strung and
  cut into 1-inch pieces
¼ small fresh cabbage, shredded
1 turnip, peeled and cut into small
  pieces
1 medium potato, peeled and cut
  into bite-size pieces
2 carrots, scraped and sliced into
  rounds
2 ears fresh corn, kernels sliced
  off cob

Sprinkle meat with Creole seasoning on all sides. On high heat, brown meat on all sides in oil and remove from pot. Lower heat and add onion, bell pepper, and celery and sauté briefly. Add garlic and sauté a minute or two. Add all tomato products, beef broth, water, and seasonings, turn heat to low, cover pot, and simmer for 1 hour.

Begin adding vegetables. First, the green beans and simmer for about 20 minutes. Then add cabbage, turnip, potatoes, and carrots and simmer for 15 minutes more or until vegetables are done. Adjust seasonings such as salt, pepper, and Creole seasoning to taste. Add corn and simmer for 10 more minutes and turn heat off. Let pot sit for an hour or more before serving.

Serves 8.

Pumpkin Soup

When the French and Spanish inhabited Louisiana, they likely got their pumpkin from the Native Americans. Pumpkins are easy to grow and their large size provides a lot of nutritious food. Actually, pumpkins are a squash and not a fruit, they taste great, and they can be prepared in many ways. However, pumpkin was not new to our settlers. The big orange globe grows equally well in the soils of France and Spain and many other countries around the world. In early New Orleans, cooks baked them in pies called tarte de citrouille, laced with brandy. They also served pumpkin as a vegetable side dish at dinner. A little cinnamon here, a pinch of nutmeg there, and pumpkin morphs into the perfect accompaniment to lamb, pork, fowl, or beef.

Creative New Orleans chefs have discovered pumpkin soup. Combined with chicken stock, cream, and seasonings of choice, it makes a hearty first course that can be glorified with crabmeat or shrimp. Some versions are a ringer for butternut squash soup because of similar textures and tastes. It also tastes similar to some carrot soups I've had. All three are a beautiful color, especially in a china soup bowl or large tureen. In the case of pumpkin, some cooks like to serve the soup right out of the hollowed-out pumpkin.

4 tbsp. butter
1 large onion, chopped
2 ribs celery, chopped
2 cloves garlic, minced
1/4 lb. andouille sausage, chopped
3 14-oz. cans chicken stock or
   equivalent homemade
5 cups pumpkin, puréed, cooked
   fresh or canned
1 large potato, peeled and cubed
   in 1/2-inch pieces
Salt and pepper to taste
1/4 tsp. nutmeg
1/8 tsp. allspice
1/4 tsp. thyme leaves, dried
1 cup heavy cream

Heat butter in large, heavy pot and sauté onion and celery until soft. Add garlic and sausage and sauté a few minutes more. Add chicken stock, pumpkin, potato, salt, pepper, nutmeg, allspice, and thyme, and simmer until potatoes are done. Purée the soup, about 1 cup at a time, in a blender. Adjust seasonings. When ready to serve, add heavy cream and heat. Do not boil. If you like the soup thinner, add a little more cream or milk to your liking. Serve in bowls with a dash of freshly grated nutmeg.

Serves 8.

Spinach-artichoke Soup

Serving a gourmet soup as a first course at a dinner party does not have to take hours to cook. Once you have your ingredients together, this one takes less than 30 minutes. You can even make it a day ahead, refrigerate, and reheat gently.

2 boxes frozen spinach	3 tbsp. flour
2 cups chicken broth, divided	2½ cups half-and-half
1 large can artichoke hearts in water	Tabasco to taste
	Salt and pepper to taste
3 tbsp. butter	Juice of ½ lemon
1 small onion, chopped	¼ cup grated Parmesan cheese

Bring spinach to boil in ½ cup water. Cover and simmer, breaking it up, and cook just until thawed. Blend in a blender with water and 1 cup of the broth. Set aside.

Drain artichokes and roughly chop. Set aside.

In a large pot, melt butter and sauté onion. Add flour and combine until smooth. Gradually add the half-and-half and cook, stirring constantly, over low heat until thickened. Add spinach and artichokes, seasonings, lemon juice, Parmesan cheese, and remaining stock and simmer for 10 minutes. Do not boil.

Serves 6 to 8.

Italian-style Cauliflower Soup

Italians do amazing things with cauliflower. The olive oil, Italian spices, pasta, and Parmesan leave no doubt what country influenced this dish. I discovered it in a little Italian restaurant in the CBD where working people ate lunch. I thought I'd died and gone to heaven. Within days, I had copied it.

1 head cauliflower	2 tsp. Italian seasoning
2 tbsp. olive oil	Salt and freshly ground pepper to taste
1 large onion, chopped	
2 stalks celery, chopped	4 oz. spaghetti
2 cloves garlic, minced	2 tbsp. chopped parsley
2 14-oz. cans chicken broth	Parmesan cheese, freshly grated, about 6 tbsp.
2 cups water	

Remove stem and leaves from cauliflower, rinse well and break into florets.

Heat olive oil in a heavy medium-size pot and sauté onion and celery. Add garlic and sauté a minute more. Add broth, water, and seasonings and bring to a boil. Add cauliflower and pasta, lower heat and simmer, covered, for about 10 minutes, or until pasta is al dente and cauliflower can be pierced easily with a knife. Add parsley.

When ready to serve, pour hot soup into bowls and place about 1 tbsp. Parmesan cheese on top of each serving.

Serves 6 to 8.

Note: If you want a creamier soup, blend about ⅔ of the soup in a blender until smooth and add to remainder of soup. In addition, ½ cup half-and-half or whipping cream can be added.

Chicken and Andouille Gumbo

Ilove seafood gumbo, but my family prefers chicken and andouille. I'll have to say their favorite is easier so I'm always game to cook up a pot. A good dark roux and lots of seasonings makes it irresistible. It's also relatively inexpensive to make, and it serves a crowd. When out-of-towners visit, it's nice to have a pot of gumbo bubbling on the stove when they arrive.

1 whole chicken, or 7 thighs
Salt, pepper, cayenne pepper, and
   Creole seasoning to taste
¾ cup vegetable oil
1 lb. andouille sausage, sliced into
   rounds
1 cup flour
1 onion

1 bell pepper
3 stalks celery
1 bunch green onions, white and
   green parts divided
4 cloves garlic, minced
2 bay leaves
2 tbsp. chopped parsley

Cut chicken into pieces. Rinse well and dry with paper towels. Sprinkle with seasonings.

Heat a tbsp. or 2 of the oil in a large, heavy pot and brown chicken pieces on all sides. Move chicken to one side, add andouille, and brown a few minutes more. Add water to cover, about 5 cups. Cover and simmer for 30 minutes. While this is cooking, chop all the vegetables. Remove chicken and andouille from pot and strain stock into a separate container and reserve.

Wipe pot clean and add remaining oil to pot; heat and stir in flour to make a roux. Stir over a medium heat until roux is medium to dark brown. Add onion, bell pepper, celery, and white part of green onions and cook until softened. Add garlic and cook another minute. Add strained stock, about 2 more cups water to reach desired consistency, bay leaves, and salt, pepper, cayenne pepper, and Creole seasonings to taste. Meanwhile, debone and skin chicken pieces, discarding bones and skin. Coarsely chop chicken and add with andouille to pot. Cover and simmer for 30 more minutes, stirring occasionally. Adjust seasonings. Shortly before removing from fire, add green onion tops and parsley. Serve in bowls over rice.

Serves 8.

Note: Oysters may be added to this gumbo, if desired. Add about 2 dozen when adding onion tops and parsley.

Chicken Noodle Soup

There is little more restorative than a good chicken noodle soup. As soon as somebody gets sick in my house, out comes the soup pot and in goes the chicken. All ages seem to warm up to this noodle soup, from grandchildren to old folks. A diet counselor once told me it was like penicillin for all its medicinal faculties. I don't think that's true, but it's a good story.

1 whole chicken	2 tbsp. butter
Water	3 carrots, scraped and cut into
1 onion, chopped	circles
½ green bell pepper, chopped	Salt and pepper to taste
½ red bell pepper, chopped	½ tsp. turmeric
3 stalks celery, chopped	½ tsp. celery salt
2 cloves garlic, minced	1 cup sliced fresh mushrooms
Freshly ground pepper	1 8-oz. package egg noodles

Place cleaned chicken in a heavy pot of water to cover. Bring to a boil.

Add ⅓ of onion, peppers, celery, and garlic to pot with chicken. Add pepper. Lower heat to a simmer, cover and cook slowly until chicken is done, about 1 hour. Turn off heat and cool chicken and stock until cool enough to handle.

Remove chicken from pot and debone, discarding skin and bones. Cut into bite-size pieces and set aside. Strain stock into a large bowl and set aside.

In the same pot, melt butter, heat and sauté remaining onion, peppers, celery, and garlic. Return stock to pot and add carrots and seasonings. Simmer, covered until carrots are done, about 20 minutes. Add chicken and mushrooms and simmer 5 minutes more. Bring heat to medium-hot and add package of egg noodles. Cook until noodles are just al dente. (They will continue to wilt in the hot soup.) Taste and adjust seasonings.

Serves 6.

White Bean Soup

The one-pot meal is a life-saver for big families. White bean soup is so rich and hearty that all you need is French bread or cornbread to make a meal. Ham or andouille seasoning is the key to this soup.

I ½ cups white beans, great northern or navy
2 tbsp. olive oil
2 carrots, chopped
2 ribs celery, chopped
I medium onion, chopped
I green bell pepper, chopped
3 cloves garlic, minced
8 cups water

I ham bone, or ½ lb. ham seasoning
3 oz. andouille sausage, cut into rounds
I tbsp. tomato paste
I tsp. oregano
Salt and pepper to taste
Flat-leaf Italian parsley, chopped
Romano cheese

Rinse and sort beans and soak for 4 hours or more, or use the quick soak technique below.

Heat olive oil in a large, heavy pot and sauté the carrots, celery, onion, and bell pepper until soft. Add garlic and sauté 1 minute more.

Strain beans and add to pot along with water. Add ham, andouille, tomato paste, oregano, salt, and pepper. Cover and simmer for about 2 hours or until beans are done. Purée a cup of the soup in a blender, or use a hand blender to purée partially for thickening. Add parsley.

When serving, sprinkle each serving with grated Romano cheese and more parsley, if desired.

Serves 8.

Quick soak: Place beans in a medium pot with water to cover by 1 inch. Bring to a boil, cover, and remove from heat. Let soak for 1 hour.

CHAPTER THREE

Salads

Shrimp-stuffed Avocados

Shrimp salad stands alone, but stuffing it into creamy avocados is the ultimate light lunch. First, the avocados must be perfectly ripened. If they are hard when you buy them, place them in a brown paper bag in a dark cabinet or drawer for a couple of days.

4 ripe avocados
2 lb. shrimp, boiled, peeled, deveined, and chopped
6 tbsp. mayonnaise, good quality or homemade
4 green onions, chopped
Salt and pepper to taste

I stalk celery, chopped
2 tbsp. lemon juice plus some for drizzling
2 tbsp. chopped parsley
½ tsp. dill weed
½ tsp. garlic powder

Slice and peel avocados. Remove seeds. An easy way to peel is to scoop the avocado out with a serving-size spoon. Drizzle with a little lemon juice to keep the avocados from turning brown. Mix all other ingredients including the 2 tbsp. of lemon juice and fill the avocado halves, spooning extra over the top.

Serves 4 as a luncheon entrée, or 8 as a dinner appetizer.

Beet Salad

Beets were not a favorite of mine until I was introduced to this simple salad. The key is making it several hours ahead of time and letting the flavors blend.

I large can beets   **2 tbsp. mayonnaise, good quality**
I small onion, sliced into rings

Drain beets. Place in small bowl and mix in onion rings. Dot with mayonnaise. Cover tightly and marinate in the refrigerator for at least 2 hours. Mix slightly to serve. Serve cold.

Serves 4 as a side dish.

Cauliflower Salad

When you go to Sicily, you realize where much of New Orleans local cooking comes from. Broccoli and cauliflower, in various colors, dominate the markets, and fava beans and cardoon, two local favorites, are in great supply. Italian salad dressing has long been an American favorite, but it doesn't have to stop with green salads. The ingredients are great over cooked, chilled vegetables such as cauliflower and broccoli. Such a salad can be prepared in minutes with amazing health benefits.

1 head cauliflower (or broccoli)	⅓ tsp. freshly ground black pepper
¼ cup extra-virgin olive oil	1 tsp. whole Italian seasoning
2 tbsp. salad, tarragon, or white wine vinegar	¼ tsp. garlic powder
	¼ tsp. sugar
1 tsp. salt	¼ tsp. celery salt

Cut away stem and green leaves of cauliflower and cut into florets. Rinse well. Place in steamer basket over boiling water, cover and cook until fork tender. Drain and cool. Cut into bite-size pieces and place in salad bowl.

Whisk together all other ingredients well, pour over cauliflower and toss. Marinate in the refrigerator for at least an hour. Toss again when ready to serve.

Serves 6 to 8.

Louisiana Citrus Salad

Use this recipe when Louisiana citrus is at its peak in the late fall. The juicy oranges will add sunshine to your green salad every time. First, peel the orange so that none of the pith remains. Then, with a very sharp knife, slice out each segment, leaving the tough membrane attached to the core. You will have nothing but succulent bites of orange to go with your favorite green salad.

½ head romaine, torn in pieces
1 cup curly endive, torn in pieces
1 cup iceberg lettuce, torn in pieces
¼ cup roasted pecan pieces*
¼ cup raisins or currants
½ cup sunflower seed kernels
⅓ cup seeded black olives, sliced in halves
½ medium red onion, sliced thin
Segments from 2 oranges
French vinaigrette**
Freshly ground black pepper

Rinse and spin dry lettuce and place in a large bowl. Do this ahead of time and place in refrigerator covered by a wet paper towel until time to serve. This will crisp up your salad. When ready to serve, add all other ingredients, toss and serve. Use the amount of vinaigrette that you prefer. Start with ½ cup. If it is enough, save the rest for another salad.

Serves 6 to 8.

*To roast: Place pecan pieces in a pan and heat in a 350-degree oven for about 10 minutes, stirring once during the roasting. When the pecans smell aromatic, they are ready. Cool.

**To make the French vinaigrette: Whisk together 1 tbsp. balsamic vinegar, 1 tbsp. salad vinegar, and 1 tbsp. Dijon mustard. Add ½ tsp. salt. Slowly drizzle 1 cup extra-virgin olive oil into the mixture, whisking constantly until an emulsion forms.

Potato Salad

I almost fainted when I heard Chef Paul Prudhomme say that potato salad was good served in gumbo. I knew about serving it on the side, but "in." I have since learned that many locals, especially in southwest Louisiana, serve it that way. To me it is still a side dish whether with gumbo, fried chicken, or barbecue. I don't like to mix mayonnaise with my gumbo. But who am I to argue with the renowned chef and half the people in south Louisiana? Everyone has his own favorite version of potato salad, however they eat it. This is mine:

6 large potatoes
6 eggs
1 medium onion, chopped
½ bell pepper, chopped
½ red bell pepper, chopped
1 large dill pickle, chopped
2 stalks celery, chopped
2 tbsp. minced flat-leaf Italian parsley

½ cup mayonnaise
2 tbsp. mustard
1 tbsp. olive oil
Salt, pepper, and Creole seasoning to taste
1 tsp. celery seed, optional
½ tsp. dill weed, optional
Paprika, optional

Boil potatoes in skins until a fork slips through easily. Remove from pot and boil eggs for 10 minutes. When both are cool enough to handle, peel, chop, and place into large bowl. Add remaining ingredients and toss until mixed well.

If you like potato salad creamier, mix while potatoes are still warm. You also can mash one or two with a fork. For non-creamy style, let potatoes cool before chopping. Serve in a pretty bowl and sprinkle with paprika and more chopped parsley, if desired.

Serves 6 to 8.

CHAPTER FOUR

Side Dishes

Stuffed Artichokes

Spring is the season for artichokes although we get them year-round from various locations. They make perfect Lenten dishes, stuffed with either seafood in a cream sauce or the traditional breadcrumbs and cheese. Long associated with Italy, they are a classic dish in New Orleans, redolent of garlic and showered with olive oil. They are a staple for St. Joseph's Day, March 19, when parades and altars laden with fish, pasta, cakes, and cookies are offered up at churches and homes, thanking St. Joseph for personal favors. Altars represent endless hours spent by loving hands shaping Italian cookies and preparing meatless dishes and desserts. Stuffed artichokes and seafood-stuffed peppers are among the specialties spread out by Italian cooks as "devotions" to the patron saint.

2 artichokes
2 cups breadcrumbs
1 cup grated Parmesan or
   Romano cheese or a mixture of
   both
6 large cloves garlic

4 green onions
10 stems parsley, leaves only
Juice of 1 lemon
Salt and Creole seasoning to taste
4 tbsp. extra-virgin olive oil, good
   quality

Cut off bottom stems of artichokes so that they sit flat. Slice off ½ inch from the top of artichokes. With scissors, cut off the sharp tip of each leaf and discard any small leaves on the bottom. Pull leaves apart to rinse artichokes thoroughly. Turn upside down to drain.

In a large bowl, combine breadcrumbs and cheese. Chop garlic, green onions, and parsley and put in a food processor to chop fine. Add to breadcrumb mixture along with lemon juice and seasonings and mix well. Use your hands if necessary.

Place an artichoke on a sheet of wax paper or a plate. Using a teaspoon, stuff each leaf beginning at the bottom. After you load a leaf, press stuffing into the leaf with back of spoon. Continue around the artichoke until all large leaves are stuffed and artichoke looks doubled in size. Use up all of the stuffing that falls on the wax paper or plate. Repeat with other artichoke.

Place a rack in the bottom of a large pot or Dutch oven and add one inch of water to the pot. Place artichokes in pot and drizzle about 2 tbsp. olive oil on each artichoke, trying to get some on each stuffed leaf. Cover pot, bring water to a boil and reduce heat to a simmer. Steam for 1 hour or until a leaf feels loose or can be easily pulled out, or until artichokes feel tender when stuck with a fork.

Serves 4 to 6 as a side dish.

Oyster Dressing

The key dish at a New Orleans Thanksgiving table is not the turkey. It is the oyster dressing. It all started back when early Creoles found themselves with the most succulent oysters this side of France and that adding them to stuffings was as delightful as adding truffles. Today, oysters dominate the holiday meals.

Most cooks combine oysters with French bread although some use them in cornbread and rice dressings. It doesn't hurt that the salty mollusks are coming into peak of season around the holidays and are usually plentiful. It is important to add enough liquid to dressings to make them moist. Keep dressings refrigerated if made ahead of time and never stuff them in poultry or meat until it is ready to go in the oven.

I long loaf French bread, stale

3 10-oz. containers (about 3 dozen medium) oysters

2 cups chicken or turkey stock, homemade or canned

I stick butter

I large onion, chopped

3 stalks celery, chopped

3 cloves garlic, minced

I bunch green onions, white and green parts separated and chopped

¼ cup parsley, chopped

Salt, pepper, Creole seasoning, and cayenne pepper to taste

Buy a po-boy loaf of French bread in paper, not plastic, several days before making your dressing and let it go stale. In a very large bowl, break up bread into small pieces and cover with strained water from the oysters and chicken stock. Let soak for 30 minutes to an hour. A good way to crumb the bread is to beat it with the side of a meat mallet while still in the paper bag.

Meanwhile, melt butter in a large skillet and sauté white onions and celery until soft, add garlic, and sauté a few minutes more. Add this, green onion tops, and parsley to the soaked bread and mix well. Check oysters to eliminate any shell, chop them, and stir into mixture. Add seasonings. Place in a 9-by-13-inch baking dish, making sure there is plenty of liquid. Add more stock or water if necessary to make dressing very moist. Bake at 400 degrees for about 45 minutes to an hour or until dressing has firmed up and is lightly brown on top.

This dressing can be stuffed into a turkey and baked, but the turkey should be stuffed at the last minute to avoid salmonella poisoning. If baked inside the turkey, make sure the dressing reaches 165 degrees.

Cajun Rice Dressing

A Louisiana dressing isn't all that simple because just about everything we cook has layers of flavors using many of the prized local ingredients. The Cajuns loved to grind everything up including the livers and gizzards. With rice growing all around them in bayou country, Cajuns found it a natural thing to stuff turkeys, usually wild, with spicy rice. For a special holiday meal, plenty of meat was added and sometimes a dressing would include giblets, ground beef, and sausage. The more meat, the merrier, but seasoning vegetables were important, too—lots of onion, garlic, peppers, and celery. All of the add-ons turned plain white rice a dark, brownish color, and it eventually became known as dirty rice. Some cooks use oysters in rice dressing. The following recipe is the way Cajuns have been doing it in the country for a long, long time.

4 cups chicken or turkey stock, homemade or canned	I large onion, chopped
2 cups rice	2 ribs celery, chopped
I lb. chicken gizzards	I bell pepper, chopped
½ lb. chicken livers	2 cloves garlic, minced
½ lb. ground beef	I bunch green onions, chopped
½ lb. ground pork	3 tbsp. parsley, chopped
½ cup oil or meat drippings	Salt, pepper, Creole seasoning, and cayenne pepper to taste

Bring chicken stock to a boil in a large saucepan. Add rice, reduce heat, cover, and simmer until done, about 20 minutes. Set aside.

Simmer chicken gizzards in water to cover until fork tender, about 30 minutes. Add livers and cook about 10 more minutes until livers are done. Drain and remove the tender meat from the gizzards, discarding the tough gristle. Place gizzard meat and livers in a food processor or grinder and process until coarse. Set aside.

In a large, heavy pot, brown the ground beef and pork, drain, and set aside. In the same pot, heat the oil and sauté onions, celery, and bell pepper until soft. Add garlic and sauté briefly. Off the heat, add rice, meat, green onions, parsley, and seasonings and toss lightly. Heat through when ready to serve. This dressing can be stuffed in a turkey and baked with the turkey. Alternatively, it can be reheated in a large baking dish in the oven or microwaved in smaller portions when ready to serve.

Serves 8 to 10.

Note: If you do not want to use gizzards, double the livers. If you do not want either one, double the ground beef and pork.

Baked Macaroni

Some people call it macaroni and cheese, or mac and cheese, but not in New Orleans. Here it is baked macaroni, a dish that is as common to home cooking as mashed potatoes or cheese grits. The definitive recipe is said to be held captive in the kitchen of Rocky and Carlo's, deep in hurricane-whipped Chalmette, but there is much speculation on how they put it together. And it's not that different from what most home cooks place on their tables at least once a week. You can fancy it up with several kinds of cheeses, but a good sharp cheddar gets the job done. What makes it distinctive is the long macaroni with the hole in the center.

1 tsp. salt, divided
½ tsp. olive oil
½ lb. long macaroni
2 eggs
2 cups whole milk
¼ tsp. cayenne pepper

½ tsp. Creole seasoning
2 cups grated sharp cheddar
 cheese
¼ cup finely grated Parmesan
 cheese

Bring a large pot of water to a boil. Add ½ tsp. salt, olive oil, and macaroni, stirring well. Boil for about 10 minutes, until al dente. Drain and set aside.

In an 7-by-11-inch or 2-qt. baking dish, beat eggs. Add milk, remaining salt, cayenne pepper, Creole seasoning, and half of both cheeses. Mix well. Add macaroni and mix well again. Top with remaining cheeses.

Bake in a preheated 350-degree oven for about 30 to 40 minutes or until bubbly.

Serves 6.

Snap Beans with New Potatoes

There are those who hate to snap beans, pick crabs, and shell peas. I think it's fun. My mother's hands were never idle, and I often picture her peeling or shelling something while conversing with a neighbor. She always knitted or crocheted while watching television. Give me the choice of a cup of picked crabmeat or a tray of boiled crabs and there is no doubt I'd rather have the whole crabs. Snapping beans is easy. Do it while you watch TV or sit on the porch in a rocking chair. This is a great side dish for a Sunday meal of pot roast or fried chicken.

3 lb. snap beans
2 lb. new potatoes
3 tbsp. olive or cooking oil
1 large onion, chopped

½ lb. ham pieces for seasoning
Salt and pepper to taste
2 tsp. sugar

Snap or cut beans into 2-inch lengths, removing ends. Rinse and drain. Peel potatoes. (Potatoes soak up seasoning better when peeled.)

Heat oil in large, heavy pot and sauté onions. Add ham and sauté for a minute or two. Add beans, salt, pepper, and sugar and turn heat to low, cover, and let beans simmer with ham and onions for about 20 minutes. During this period, beans should release some liquid and cook down a bit. If not, add a little water and continue simmering, covered, for about 40 more minutes. When beans cook in their own juices, their flavor is more intense than when they are boiled in water.

After beans have cooked for an hour, add potatoes and enough water just to cover the vegetables. Continue simmering, covered, until the potatoes are done, about 35 to 40 minutes.

This serves a crowd. For 4 people, cut recipe in half.

Pumpkin Casserole

When we think of pumpkin, we almost always think of pumpkin pie. Actually, it makes an excellent vegetable side dish for dinner. A little cinnamon here, a pinch of nutmeg there, and pumpkin morphs into the perfect accompaniment to lamb, pork, fowl, or beef. There are a full range of uses for the pumpkin, which can play an important role in healthful diets. Pumpkins are rich in vitamin A and potassium and are high in fiber. Better yet, they are low in calories and devoid of fat.

4 strips bacon	Salt and pepper
1 medium onion, chopped	¼ tsp. cayenne pepper
4 green onions, chopped	2 eggs, beaten
4 cups pumpkin, puréed, cooked	¼ cup half-and-half
fresh or canned	1 cup Swiss cheese, grated
2 tbsp. honey	¼ cup breadcrumbs, seasoned
½ tsp. allspice	2 tbsp. butter, cut into bits
½ tsp. cinnamon	

In a large, heavy skillet, fry bacon until crisp. Remove, drain, and reserve bacon. Leave 2 tbsp. bacon grease in skillet and sauté the onions. Add pumpkin, honey, and seasonings and simmer for 15 minutes. Remove from heat. Mix eggs with half-and-half and stir into the pumpkin mixture. Place mixture in a casserole dish. Top with Swiss cheese and then with breadcrumbs and dot with butter. Bake in a preheated 350-degree oven for 45 minutes. When almost done, crumble bacon and sprinkle on top.

Serves 6 to 8 as side dish.

Candied Sweet Potatoes

If you're looking for a great dish to go with pork, try this simple old-fashioned recipe. Sweet potatoes are a major crop for Louisiana, and there are so many good ways to fix them. A baked sweet potato oozing in butter is hard to beat, but this crispy version is close.

2 sweet potatoes
3 tbsp. butter
⅓ cup light brown sugar

¼ tsp. salt
¼ tsp. cinnamon

Peel and slice sweet potatoes into ¼-inch rounds. Place in pot, cover with water, and cook until done, about 15 minutes. Drain.

In a large skillet, melt butter and sauté sweet potato slices in a single layer until they are partly browned on both sides. Sprinkle with sugar, salt, and cinnamon. Cook, covered, and stir carefully until sugar has melted and potatoes are coated.

Serves 4.

Asparagus with Hollandaise Sauce

Spring calls for walks in the park, bouquets of flowers, and asparagus with hollandaise sauce. Along with new potatoes, fresh tomatoes, and garden peas, asparagus is one of the often-sought vegetables to accompany Easter, Mother's Day, and other springtime occasions. There is no tastier way to serve it than with a hollandaise sauce.

1 lb. fresh asparagus	2 sticks butter
Salt	2 tsp. lemon juice
2 egg yolks	Salt and white pepper

Rinse asparagus and snap off the tough ends, about 1 inch. Place in a glass baking dish with a splash of water (enough just to cover bottom of dish) and microwave on high for a couple of minutes. Test for doneness by sticking a fork in the large end. When the fork slides through yet the asparagus is still bright green and crispy, asparagus is done. The length of cooking depends on the size of asparagus.

To make the hollandaise: See index for Hollandaise Sauce.

Serves 6.

Southern-style Greens

My mother always said that greens are better after the first frost. We don't get many frosts in New Orleans, but greens are often available in the markets and grocery stores. A fall vegetable, greens are tenderer when young although taste can develop later. I go by looks. If they look fresh and pretty, I buy them. Add a little pork seasoning and by all means serve them with cornbread.

2 large bunches mustard, turnip, or collard greens, or mixed	¼ lb. tasso, ham, or other pork seasoning meat
2 tbsp. vegetable oil	Salt and pepper to taste
1 large onion, chopped	1 tsp. sugar

Trim greens of heavy or tough stems. Wash greens well by filling a sink with cold water and swishing them around in the water. Let the water drain off. Repeat twice. Or, wash them leaf by leaf under the faucet. Drain.

On a cutting board, cut greens roughly with a large, heavy knife. If using turnip greens, remove turnips, peel and cut into ½-inch slices.

In a large heavy pot, heat oil and sauté onion until soft. Add seasoning meat and sauté for a couple of minutes. Add greens and sprinkle with seasonings. If not all greens will fit into pot at once, cover the amount that will fit and cook over medium heat until wilted, about 10 minutes. Add other greens, stir, cover, and cook over low heat for 30 to 45 minutes, stirring occasionally. Greens will make their own juice. In the last half of cooking time, you may want to add up to 1 cup of water if greens appear to be drying out. Greens should be tender but not overcooked.

If turnips are used, place them on top of the greens during the last 15 minutes of cooking. Sprinkle with a little seasoning and they will steam tender.

Serve with cornbread and green onions on the side.

Serves 4 to 6.

Garden Peas with Mushrooms and Pearl Onions

My mother loved to shell peas and butterbeans. Some of them grew along the fence in our backyard and others in the huge garden my father always grew. It was simple cooking, just simmering them in a little water with a piece of ham or bacon. But when she added cornbread, a few sliced homegrown tomatoes, and relish made from other fresh vegetables, you hardly needed an entrée. Few of us have these in gardens, but farmers' markets sometimes sell them. Look for them at roadside stands. Barring that, the frozen product is nearly as good. Dress them up with mushrooms and pearl onions and you have a holiday side dish.

2 tbsp. butter
1 heaping cup (about 5 oz.) pearl
  onions
½ cup mushrooms, white,
portobello, or shiitake (or
  mixed), sliced, or whole if small
1 lb. fresh or frozen green peas
Salt and pepper

Melt butter in a medium saucepan. Trim ends and peel onions and sauté in butter over low heat, covered, for about 10 minutes, turning occasionally. Add mushrooms and sauté for 1 minute over medium heat. Add 1 cup water, bring to a boil, and add peas. Reduce heat to a simmer and cook until peas are done but still bright green, about 15 minutes. Season to taste with salt and pepper.

New Potatoes in Cream Sauce

Side dishes are as important as entrées in the makeup of a meal. After all, what is steak without the potato, pizza minus salad, turkey sans dressing? Spring gardens offer the best possibilities—fresh peas, asparagus, strawberries, and new potatoes. I've always felt that small, tender new potatoes are a sure sign of spring.

2 lb. new potatoes	3½ cups milk
1 stick butter	Salt and white pepper to taste
8 tbsp. flour	

Peel potatoes. When freshly harvested from a garden, the peeling will actually rub off with a towel. Boil in salted water until a fork inserts easily. Do not overcook.

Melt butter in small saucepan. Remove from heat and stir in flour until mixture is completely smooth. Add milk gradually, stirring until each addition is blended well. Return to heat and simmer, stirring constantly, until sauce is thickened. Do not boil. Add salt and white pepper to taste. Add potatoes and stir to coat.

Serves 6.

Potatoes au Gratin, Home-style

This steakhouse favorite goes well with any grilled meats and comple-ments holiday dinners. It is especially good with a standing rib roast.

4 large russet potatoes
2 medium onions
4 tbsp. butter
4 tbsp. flour

2 cups whole milk or half-and-half
Salt and pepper to taste
2 cups grated extra-sharp
    cheddar cheese

Peel and slice potatoes and onions $1/8$ to $1/4$ inch thick.

Bring a medium-large pot of water to a boil, place potatoes and onions in water, lower heat to a simmer and cook until potatoes are fork tender.

Meanwhile, melt butter in a small saucepan. Remove from heat and stir in flour until smooth. Gradually add milk or cream until thoroughly mixed and smooth. Return to low heat and stir constantly until sauce is thickened, season to taste with salt and pepper.

Drain potatoes and onions when done. Butter a 9-by-13-inch dish and line with half the potatoes and onions. Pour half the cream sauce over and layer the remaining potatoes and onions. Pour remaining sauce on top and cover with cheese. Bake in a preheated 350-degree oven until bubbly, about 30 to 40 minutes.

Serves 6 to 8.

Creamed Potatoes with Horseradish

Just when I thought creamed potatoes couldn't get any better, along came horseradish. This pairing came one night in Florida when a hurricane threatened. With plans cancelled at a food writers' conference, we cooked our own meal. A fellow food writer spiked the potatoes with a hefty addition of horseradish. I've been doing it ever since.

6 large potatoes, russet or red
½ stick butter
1 tbsp. horseradish, fresh
    preferred*

Salt, pepper, and Creole seasoning
    to taste
1 to 2 cups whole milk or half-
    and-half

Peel potatoes and cut into large chunks. Boil in water to cover until fork tender. Drain.

In a mixer, cream potatoes until there are no lumps. Add butter and mix some more. Add horseradish and seasonings. Add milk or cream gradually until desired consistency is reached. Some people like potatoes firm while others like them creamy. Use the amount of liquid that you prefer.

Serves 6 to 8.

*Fresh horseradish is sold in the refrigerated case of grocery stores.

Rosemary Potatoes

This side dish goes with everything, whether it's barbecue, lamb, steak, fish, or chicken. Rosemary is the easiest herb to grow, and one little plant will sometimes last for years in a pot on the patio. I love this dish in the springtime when the new potatoes are just right.

2 lb. small red potatoes, cut in half with peeling on
1 tsp. salt
1 tsp. freshly ground pepper

1 tsp. Creole seasoning
4 tbsp. fresh rosemary, chopped
4 tbsp. extra-virgin olive oil
1 large onion, sliced into rings

Preheat oven to 400 degrees. Place potatoes in the bottom of a baking pan. In a small bowl, mix salt, pepper, Creole seasoning, and rosemary. Sprinkle half the mixture over the potatoes and drizzle with 2 tbsp. of the olive oil. Bake for 20 minutes. Scatter onion rings over the potatoes, top with remaining seasoning, and sprinkle remaining olive oil. Bake for another 30 minutes or until potatoes are done.

Serves 6.

Grits Soufflé

When I moved to New Orleans decades ago, a friend gave me a recipe that she called baked grits. Because you separated the eggs and whipped the whites, I changed the name to grits soufflé. One of my specialties was grillades with grits soufflé, and while just plain grits are fine with grillades, this version is all the better. Its lightness gives a special texture that complements the rich gravy of the grillades.

3 cups cooked grits*	**½ stick butter**
3 eggs, separated	**Salt to taste**
¾ cup milk	

Preheat oven to 350 degrees. Combine grits with beaten egg yolks, milk, melted butter, and salt. Beat egg whites until stiff and fold into grits. Place in a large, greased casserole dish and bake for 1 hour. This dish is best served immediately.

Serves 6.

*To make 3 cups of grits: Bring 3 cups of salted water to a boil and add 1 cup of quick grits, stirring constantly while adding. Turn heat to low, cover, and cook according to package directions.

Garlic Cheese Grits

One of the last remaining differences between northerners and southerners in the United States is the love of grits. Some northerners hang on to their potatoes while most southerners can't go long without grits and rice. A big breakfast, the kind you have once a week, demands grits, but I like them as a side to many dinner entrées. Grillades require grits, of course, but grits are equally good with pork chops or roast beef and gravy, especially with a tinge of cheese and garlic.

I cup quick grits
4 cups water
I tsp. salt
½ stick butter
I 6-oz. roll garlic cheese, cut into small chunks

4 oz. sharp cheddar cheese, cut into small chunks
I tbsp. Worcestershire
2 eggs, beaten
½ cup milk

Stir grits into boiling, salted water. Lower heat to a simmer, cover, and cook until done, about 10 minutes. Remove from heat and stir in remaining ingredients. Place in a 2-qt. casserole or baking dish and bake in a preheated 350-degree oven for 20 to 30 minutes, until nearly firm in center. Let sit for 10 minutes while it continues to firm and serve.

Serves 6 to 8.

Corn Maque Choux

I grew up on fresh creamed corn, but it was not until I moved to Louisiana that I learned to put the bell peppers, onions, and other seasonings in it. What a good example of the difference in Deep South and Creole cooking! The beauty of the dish is scraping the cobs and letting the natural cornstarch thicken the dish. I add a smidgeon of sugar but prefer the fresh taste of the corn without the sweetness used in canned versions. Using red as well as green peppers makes it a beautifully colored side dish.

8 ears corn
2 tbsp. corn oil
I medium onion, chopped
I green bell pepper, chopped
I red bell pepper, chopped

I clove garlic, minced
½ cup water
I tsp. sugar
Salt and pepper to taste

Shuck corn, removing silks, rinse, and drain. With a sharp knife, slice kernels off the cobs about ⅔ of the way through. With a dull knife, scrape the cobs, getting all of the remaining juice from them. This is best done in a large bowl, as corn will splatter. Set aside.

In a large, heavy skillet, sauté the vegetables in the oil for several minutes. Add the corn, water, sugar, salt, and pepper, cover, and simmer over medium heat for about 20 minutes until corn has thickened. Stir several times during cooking to keep mixture from sticking. Adjust seasonings and serve.

Serves 6 to 8.

Cornbread

Some people I know love to eat leftover cornbread with buttermilk mixed together in a bowl or glass. I have never done this because I don't drink buttermilk. I love it for cooking and making salad dressings, but I never acquired a taste for drinking it. However, I believe that two things absolutely demand it in their cooking, and they are biscuits and cornbread. The flavors are so much better when buttermilk is used. Cornbread also requires just the right balance of salt and sugar. Serve it plain with vegetables, or dress it up Mexican style to go with soups.

2 tbsp. vegetable oil	Pinch baking soda
I egg	½ tsp. salt
I cup corn meal, white or yellow	I tsp. sugar or I envelope Splenda
2½ tsp. baking powder	I cup buttermilk

Preheat oven to 425 degrees. Add oil to an 8-inch round or square metal pan and heat in oven while you mix the other ingredients.

In a medium bowl, beat egg with a whisk. Add all dry ingredients and mix well. Add buttermilk and mix. Remove pan from oven, pour oil into corn meal mixture, and stir quickly. Pour back into pan and bake for 20 minutes or just until firm. If top isn't browned, place under broiler to brown. Cut into squares or pie shapes.

Serves 6.

For Mexican corn bread: Add ½ cup canned or cooked corn kernels, 1 chopped jalapeno pepper, and ½ cup sharp cheddar cheese after you add the buttermilk.

CHAPTER FIVE

Entrées

Boiled Crabs

There's no better outing for a family with young kids than a trip to the bayou or lake to catch crabs. Before the crawfish boil became the standard backyard boil, locals were filling their boiling pots with blue crabs, a year-round harvest in Louisiana. Blue crabs are in peak season from May to October, and Louisiana is the number two producer of crabs in the country. It's the flavor of the blue crab that sets it apart, and in the peak of season, the yellow fat inside is the ultimate sauce to match its sweet, succulent taste. The same ingredients used in crawfish boils—potatoes, corn, and onions—go well with crabs.

2 bags crab boil
1 tbsp. cayenne pepper or to taste
3 tbsp. salt or to taste

2 lemons, cut in half
2 dozen live blue crabs

Fill a large pot ⅔ full with water. This can be done indoors or outdoors, using about 3 gallons water. Bring to a boil, drop in all seasonings, squeezing lemons into water, and simmer for 30 minutes. Bring back to a boil and plunge crabs into water. When the water returns to a boil, boil for 15 minutes. Turn off fire and soak for 10 minutes.

Serves 4 to 6.

Note: If adding vegetables, add small potatoes 5 minutes before adding crabs, medium onions with the crabs, and corn in the last minute of boiling.

Crab Cakes

Crab cakes are now all over the menus of restaurants everywhere, but when it comes to crabs, chefs don't have anything on the home cooks who used to pick their crabs and stuff the shells for a Friday night supper on the bayou. Somebody in the family probably caught those crabs earlier in the day so the crabmeat was fresher than you can get it in a restaurant.

That was and still is the beauty of home cooking in Louisiana. You just can't beat the fresh ingredients we have in the waters all around us. In the city where few of us catch anything ourselves, we have only to stop in a seafood store to buy crabs, shrimp, and oysters that slept in the marshes last night. For crabs, the peak season is May through October, and Louisiana is second only to the Chesapeake Bay area in the production of blue crabs.

Here we appreciate the whole crab. None of that throwing away the delicious yellow fat in the center. Nor would we discriminate against the claw meat or back fin meat as inferior. It's just used in different ways. Many cooks prefer claw meat for stuffing crabs because the meat is sweeter, not to mention less expensive.

In the early days, Creoles called crab cakes croquettes. They contained essentially the same ingredients except for the Creole seasoning that we rely on so heavily today. Instead, they used fresh thyme, parsley, and bay leaf. Croquettes were fried while stuffed crabs were baked. A dish called deviled crabs was stuffed with a similar mixture but also included hard-boiled eggs, cream, and nutmeg. These were finished off either by baking or frying. Another variation of the stuffed crab/crab cake is the crab ball, a golf-ball size version that sometimes fills in on a seafood platter. Like the deviled crabs, they can be either fried or baked.

In my mind, the crab cake should be ninety percent lump crabmeat with just enough breadcrumbs to hold it together. Standing unabashed and alone, it relies on pure taste to make its mark. The stuffed crab, on the other hand, is an interesting item on a plate, all dressed up in its bright red armor. A little more dressing or filling can be tolerated as long as the sweet crabmeat and proper seasonings shine through.

If you want to stuff the crab shells, then you'll have to buy some boiled crabs and pick them yourself. You can always save a few from a crab boil. If you're shell-less, then go with the crab cake. It's easy, delicious, and elegant for a dinner party.

I lb. lump crabmeat (back fin or jumbo)
I large egg, beaten
I ½ tbsp. mayonnaise
I tsp. Worcestershire sauce
I tsp. dry mustard
I tsp. Creole seasoning

Salt and pepper to taste
2 tbsp finely chopped parsley
I ½ slices bread, toasted and crumbled in a food processor
½ cup vegetable oil
½ cup breadcrumbs, seasoned

Carefully check crabmeat for shell. Spread it out on a plate or waxed paper and use your fingertips to feel for shells. Try not to break it apart too much. Set aside.

In a large bowl, combine the egg, mayonnaise, Worcestershire, dry mustard, seasonings, and parsley. Stir in the crumbled bread slice.

Divide mixture into 6 portions and shape each into a patty about 1 inch thick. In a large skillet, heat vegetable oil to medium-hot.

Roll crab cakes lightly in breadcrumbs and sauté about 3 minutes on each side or until golden brown. Remove and drain on paper towels.

Crab cakes can be served alone or with a sauce such as tartar or rémoulade.

Serves 3 as an entrée, 6 as an appetizer.

Stuffed Crabs

I thought crab cakes were an invention of the modern world until I realized we'd been making them all along. Here in Louisiana, ours were a little different. We just stuffed them into crab shells. What I like about the stuffed crab is its jazzy presentation on the plate. Seafood platters used to always contain them though many have now gone to the crab ball for obvious reasons. It is easier. Many cooks prefer claw meat for stuffing crabs because the meat is sweeter, not to mention less expensive. Stuffed crabs can also be lower in fat than the crab cake because they are baked and the crab cake is usually fried or sautéed.

I dozen boiled crabs
4 tbsp. butter, divided
½ cup onion, finely chopped
¼ cup celery, finely chopped
¼ cup bell pepper, finely chopped
2 cloves garlic, minced
2 tbsp. finely chopped parsley

I egg, beaten
½ tsp. each salt, pepper, and
    Creole seasoning
I tbsp. lemon juice
I cup plus ¼ cup breadcrumbs,
    seasoned

Pick crabs, saving meat and fat. Clean the back shells of 6 to 8 crabs, depending on size, discarding all else. Set aside.

Melt 2 tbsp. butter in a large, heavy skillet and sauté the onion, celery, and bell pepper until soft. Add garlic and sauté briefly.

In a medium bowl, mix crabmeat and fat, parsley, egg, onion mixture, seasonings, lemon juice, and 1 cup of breadcrumbs. Divide into 6 to 8 portions. Stuff mixture into shells and top with remaining breadcrumbs. Dot with remaining 2 tbsp. of butter, cut into bits.

Bake in a preheated 350-degree oven until stuffed crabs are nicely browned, about 20 to 30 minutes.

Serves 6 to 8.

Eggplant Medallions with Crabmeat Béchamel

Fresh Louisiana vegetables and local seafood are a marriage made in heaven. Eggplants, for example, scream for shrimp or crabmeat. Stuffing is one way to combine them and a good way, indeed. Here is a killer entrée made for a dinner party.

1 large eggplant	3 tbsp. olive oil or more if needed
1 cup flour plus 4 tbsp.	4 tbsp. butter
1 egg	3 cups half-and-half
1 tbsp. milk	Salt and white pepper to taste
1½ cups breadcrumbs, Italian seasoned	1 lb. lump crabmeat
	2 tbsp. capers

Peel and slice eggplant into ½-inch medallions. Salt and place slices between two plates for 30 minutes. Pour off water and pat dry. Line up 3 small bowls. In the first, put 1 cup flour mixed liberally with salt and pepper. In the next, beat the egg and milk together, and in the last, the breadcrumbs.

Heat olive oil in a wide non-stick skillet. When medium-hot, dip eggplant slices first into flour, then egg mixture, then breadcrumbs and brown on both sides, turning frequently, until done. Take out on paper towels to drain and keep warm.

In a medium saucepan, melt butter. Remove from fire and stir in 4 tbsp. flour. Mix until smooth. Gradually add half-and-half and mix until smooth. Return to low heat and, stirring constantly, cook until sauce begins to bubble and is thickened. Do not boil. Remove from fire. Add salt and pepper, crabmeat, and capers.

To serve, place 2 eggplant medallions on each plate and spoon crabmeat mixture over.

Serves 4.

Stuffed Eggplant

Being my favorite vegetable, eggplant can't get any better than when mixed with shrimp and crabmeat. My introduction was at Galatoire's when I discovered oysters Rockefeller and stuffed eggplant on the same day. That was just after I met a friend under the clock at Holmes-zes, and I thought I had died and gone to heaven. The great thing about New Orleans is that I can still go to that restaurant and get the same great dishes. Meanwhile I've learned to make them at home. It's not that I cook gourmet dishes all the time. I don't. Still, it's nice to experiment, and I've done my share of that since I discovered the city of good food.

3 medium eggplants
2 tbsp. olive oil
I large onion, chopped
½ bell pepper, chopped
I stalk celery, chopped
2 cloves garlic, minced
2 tsp. Italian seasoning
½ tsp. each salt and pepper
I lb. shrimp, peeled and deveined

½ cup breadcrumbs, Italian
    seasoned, divided
2 tbsp. chopped flat-leafed parsley
I lb. lump crabmeat, picked over
    for shells but kept in chunks
2 tbsp. butter, cut into very small
    cubes
Parmesan cheese, freshly grated

In a large pot of boiling, salted water, cook eggplants until a sharp knife slips through easily at the center. Cool enough to handle and slice in halves lengthwise. Scoop out eggplant pulp, leaving a shell about ¼ inch thick. Chop the pulp into small cubes, place in a bowl, and set aside.

In a large skillet or pot, heat olive oil and sauté onion, bell pepper, and celery until soft. Add garlic and sauté a minute more. Add Italian seasoning, salt, and pepper.

Mix in the eggplant pulp and shrimp. Add a little water—about 2 tbsp.—if needed to make a loose consistency, cover, and simmer for 5 minutes. Fold in ¼ cup breadcrumbs and parsley. Then very carefully fold in crabmeat keeping the chunks intact. Stuff mixture into shells and sprinkle with remaining breadcrumbs, dot with butter, and sprinkle lightly with Parmesan cheese. Just before serving, bake in a preheated 350-degree oven for 30 minutes.

Serves 6.

Trout Meunière

Our fishing grounds are some of the best in the world for the prized speckled trout. In fact, the black-spotted silver fish are so highly regarded for their taste and texture that they have long dominated the menus at fine restaurants in New Orleans, sharing space only with the delicate flounder and pompano. That was until gillnet restrictions choked out many commercial fishermen from catching trout and some other fish and chefs began promoting underutilized species such as black drum and sheepshead.

Without a doubt, one dish that helped move New Orleans into the culinary spotlight of the world was trout meunière, a favorite of locals for most of the twentieth century. A simple preparation, it requires sautéing a floured trout fillet in butter, adding lemon juice to the skillet, and pouring the lightly browned butter over the fish. Sadly, the fish markets are no longer filled with piles of fresh whole fish stacked on ice. Some sell tilapia, black drum, and red snapper. And, now and then, the local speckled trout will turn up. Summer is the season to be on the lookout for speckled trout.

1 stick (8 tbsp.) butter
4 8-oz. speckled trout fillets
2 cups flour, seasoned liberally
   with salt, pepper, and Creole
   seasoning

Juice of 2 lemons
Parsley

Melt butter in a large skillet. Dredge fish fillets in seasoned flour and sauté over medium heat until browned, about 6 minutes on each side. Place fillets on plates and keep warm. Add lemon juice to skillet to make sauce. Stir until thickened and pour over fish. Garnish with chopped parsley.

Serves 4.

Whole Fish Creole

We hear a lot about red fish courtbouillon, a dish in which you cook pieces of fish in a spicy tomato sauce. It is truly a classic Creole dish, but I prefer to cook the fish whole with the Creole sauce spread over it. There's something about cooking anything with the bone in that makes it tastier, I believe. It also has a better, moister texture as long as you don't over-cook it. In my opinion, the biggest mistake that can be made in cooking fish is to overcook it. It goes from succulent to dried-out, flaky to rubbery, in no time at all. A number of firm-fleshed fish can be used in the recipe, and you can still serve the rice that goes with courtbouillon with this wonderful sauce.

- 3- to 5-lb. red snapper, mangrove, or red fish, cleaned and scaled but left whole
- 1 tbsp. Creole seasoning
- 2 tbsp. canola or olive oil
- 1 medium bell pepper, chopped
- 1 large onion, chopped
- 2 ribs celery, chopped
- 3 cloves garlic, minced
- 1 14.5-oz. can diced plum tomatoes
- 1 15-oz. can tomato sauce
- Salt, pepper, and cayenne pepper to taste
- 1 tsp. sugar
- 1 tsp. Italian seasoning
- 2 bay leaves
- 2 tbsp. lemon juice

Sprinkle Creole seasoning all over fish and into cavity. Place fish in large baking pan and preheat oven to 375 degrees.

In a skillet, sauté in oil the bell pepper, onion, celery, and garlic until soft. Add tomatoes, tomato sauce, seasonings, and lemon juice. Simmer, covered, for about 30 minutes. Pour sauce over fish, placing some under the fish and in its cavity. Bake for 30 minutes to 1 hour (depending on size of fish) or until fish is flaky and white (no longer opaque) at its thickest point. Spoon sauce over fish several times during baking. You may need to add a little water (half cup at a time) to the pan several times during the baking to keep sauce from burning. This makes a good gravy.

To serve, place fish on a serving platter topped with the sauce. Garnish with lemon slices and parsley sprigs. This makes an impressive presentation. Serve with white rice.

Serves 4 to 6.

Pecan-crusted Catfish

A mande is the French word for almond, and trout amandine is a forerunner to trendy versions of nut-crusted fish. Today, chefs plaster fish fillets with pecans, pistachios, almonds, and hazelnuts, using various fish from catfish to amberjack. It's the crunch that counts.

The most readily available fish in markets today is the farm-raised catfish. Fresh and frozen, they are a good product and lend themselves to many styles of cooking. Whatever the recipe, it's an easy catch for the busy cook.

I cup pecan pieces
I cup flour, seasoned liberally
   with salt, pepper, and Creole
   seasoning
I egg

½ cup milk
½ cup breadcrumbs
4 6- to 8-oz. catfish fillets
I stick (8 tbsp.) butter

Spread pecan pieces in a small pan and toast in a 400-degree oven for about 10 minutes until fragrant. Chop a little finer.

Place seasoned flour in a wide bowl or plate. In a second wide bowl, beat egg and add milk. In a third plate, place breadcrumbs mixed with pecans.

Heat butter to medium heat in a large non-stick skillet. Dredge each fillet into flour mixture first, and then egg wash and finally breadcrumb mixture. Sauté for 6 to 8 minutes on each side or until done and nicely browned. If the fillets are browning too quickly, turn more frequently.

Serves 4.

Sesame-crusted Grilled Tuna

Fresh tuna is in great demand these days, and grocery stores make it available from the cold waters of the north. The Gulf of Mexico is another source, and you might find the local catch in some seafood stores or from a fisherman if you are lucky enough to know one. This recipe is a takeoff on one that Commander's Palace does. Theirs is served on a salad and is pan seared. This version stands alone and is seared on the grill.

3 tbsp. sesame seeds
2 tbsp. freshly ground pepper
1 ½ tsp. salt

3 tbsp. honey
4 tuna steaks, about 2 inches
    thick and 4 to 5 oz. each

Mix sesame seeds, pepper, and salt in a small bowl. Brush both sides of tuna steaks with honey and dip into sesame seeds and pepper mixture to coat the tops and bottoms of steaks. Sear on a preheated, hot charcoal or gas grill for 2 or 3 minutes on each side to serve rare, or longer if preferred.

Serves 4.

Red Fish Courtbouillon

The availability of red fish has diminished since overfishing made it off-limits. However, the Louisiana coast is blessed with so many succulent fish that substitutions can be just as good. Black fish, for one, is a member of the same drum family as the red fish. Other firm-fleshed fish that cook well in this tomato-based sauce are red snapper and amberjack. Farm-raised catfish are also an option. The classic French court-bouillon is an aromatic stock only lightly seasoned and containing wine, lemon, or vinegar in which various fish and some meats are cooked. In Louisiana, a spicy red sauce starts with a roux. You might find a red fish or two from Texas in some seafood markets.

1½ lb. fillets of firm-fleshed fish
    such as red fish, black drum, or
    red snapper
3 tbsp. butter
3 tbsp. flour
1 large onion, chopped
1 bell pepper, chopped
1 stalk celery, chopped
3 green onions, chopped
3 cloves garlic, crushed
1 1-lb., 12-oz. can crushed
    tomatoes

1 10-oz. can Rotel tomatoes
2 bay leaves
1 tbsp. sugar
1 tbsp. thyme leaves
Salt and cayenne pepper to taste
½ cup red wine
1 tbsp. Worcestershire sauce
Juice of ½ lemon
2 tbsp. chopped parsley

Cut fish into 2-inch chunks and set aside in the refrigerator. In a large, heavy pot, make a roux with butter and flour. When roux is light to medium brown, add onion, bell pepper, celery, and green onions and sauté until soft. Add garlic and sauté another minute. Add remaining ingredients except parsley and cook for 15 minutes. Add fish and cook for 10 minutes more. When done, stir in parsley. Serve over white, fluffy rice.

Serves 4 to 6.

Note: When in season, 6 large, red-ripe Creole tomatoes can be used instead of canned.

Grilled Snapper

Fish on the grill gives that outdoor flavor to one of the most healthful of entrées. My favorite is red snapper, but redfish or black drum will do equally well. Be sure to get firm-fleshed fish and the freshest you can find. Fewer seafood dealers are offering fresh whole fish, but there are still a few around.

One of the problems with grilling fish on an outdoor rig is that the flesh of the fish can stick to the grill. First, clean the grill well and spray it with cooking spray. I like to leave the skin and scales on a fillet in order to use its armor as a cooking utensil. You still get the charcoal flavor if you cover the grill and let the smoke flow over it. By first placing it flesh side down for a few minutes, you will get grill markings as well as direct flavor from the coals.

1 3-lb. red snapper (red fish or black drum also can be used)	Garlic powder
Creole seasoning	Juice of ½ lemon
Salt and freshly ground black pepper	1 tbsp. Worcestershire sauce
	2 tbsp. butter, melted

Cut fish in half, removing head and center bone. You can have this done by your seafood vendor. Leave skin and scales in tact to serve as a cooking utensil and hold fish together.

Light a charcoal or gas grill and heat to medium-hot. Make sure the grill is scraped clean and oil it with non-stick cooking spray.

Meanwhile, sprinkle cut sides of fish with Creole seasoning, salt, pepper, and garlic power. Mix lemon juice, Worcestershire, and butter for a basting sauce.

Brush fish lightly with basting sauce and place on grill about 6 to 8 inches above coals, cut sides down, and grill for about 3 minutes, just long enough to put grill marks on the fish. Carefully turn with a long spatula and place the fish skin side down. Baste liberally with butter mixture. Cover grill and cook until fish flakes, basting occasionally. To determine doneness, cut into thickest part with a knife. Fish is done when white and not opaque. This should take about 10 minutes.

Fish can be served on skin, or skin and scales can be removed by running a sharp knife between the flesh and skin.

Serves 2.

Stuffed Mirlitons

Having a mirliton vine in your backyard is as common as growing tomatoes or bell peppers in New Orleans. The best part is they require almost no attention and just grow and grow and grow. The timing of these friendly fall vegetable pears, nicknamed for their shape, is perfect for cooks who like to get a head start on holiday cooking, tucking away traditional dishes in their freezers to lighten the load when chaos arrives. In Mexico and the American Southwest, they are called chayote and are eaten differently from the way we prepare ours. Only in New Orleans are they called mirlitons, pronounced meer-lee-tawn in French but mel-a-tahn in Louisiana. Cajuns call them vegetable pears, and I am told that they are referred to as mango squash in other locations. With so many noms de plume, it's no wonder that this tropical plant is foreign to most American cooks.

The mild flavor of a mirliton makes it a match for all sorts of ingredients. Shrimp, ham, sausage, ground meat, and crabmeat complement it well in casseroles or stuffed shells. Some cooks smother it with onions, and it pickles as easily as cucumbers. Actually, the mirliton is a member of the cucumber family with a crisp flesh and the subtle flavor of a squash. Like cucumbers and squash, it is part of the giant gourd family.

Local chefs take it to the max with dishes like mirliton-shrimp Napoleon and shrimp-mirliton soup, but the favorite at-home preparation by far is stuffing. Many cooks put the stuffing into a casserole dish rather than back into the mirliton shells. Either way, they freeze well and can be saved for that important Thanksgiving or Christmas meal.

4 mirlitons

5 tbsp. butter, divided

1 medium onion, chopped

1 bell pepper, chopped

1 stalk celery, chopped

2 cloves garlic, minced

1 lb. small to medium shrimp,
     peeled and deveined

¼ lb. smoked ham, chopped fine

Pinch cayenne

Salt and pepper to taste

1 tsp. Italian seasoning

1 cup Italian breadcrumbs,
     divided

2 tbsp. chopped parsley

¼ cup grated Parmesan cheese

In a large pot of water, boil whole mirlitons until just tender. A knife should slide through, but pulp should not be overcooked. When cool, cut in half, remove and discard seeds, and scoop out meat, leaving shell thick enough to stuff, about $1/4$ inch thick. A grapefruit spoon works well for this. Mash mirliton pulp with a fork, or chop briefly in a food processor. Set aside both pulp and shells.

Melt 3 tbsp. of the butter in a large skillet and sauté onions, bell pepper, and celery until transparent. Add garlic and sauté for 5 minutes more. Add shrimp, ham, reserved mirliton pulp, cayenne, salt, pepper, and Italian seasoning and cook, stirring, for 5 or so minutes, or until shrimp are pink. Remove from heat and add $3/4$ cup of the breadcrumbs and parsley. Mix well.

Divide stuffing equally in prepared mirliton shells and top with remaining breadcrumbs. Sprinkle with Parmesan cheese and dot with remaining 2 tbsp. of butter cut into $1/4$-inch cubes. (At this point, stuffed mirlitons may be wrapped in freezer wrap or placed in plastic freezer bags and frozen.)

To bake: Place freshly prepared or thawed mirlitons on baking sheet and bake at 350 degrees until tops are browned and mirlitons are heated through, about 30 minutes.

Serves 4 as an entrée, 8 as a side dish.

Barbecued Shrimp

Ionce covered courts for *The States-Item* when the Louisiana Supreme Court was still on Loyola Avenue. In making the rounds on my beat, I sometimes happened into the high court's clerk's office around lunchtime. The justices had their own cook, and if I wandered into the adjoining kitchen, he occasionally would ask me if I wanted to taste something. My lucky day was when the aroma of barbecued shrimp was wafting through the halls of justice and I sat down just as they were coming out of the oven. Boy oh boy! Were they ever delicious! I have long since forgotten the cook's name, but he gave me his secrets. Most importantly, you must leave the heads on the shrimp. The fat in the heads is a main ingredient. Secondly, you don't use any barbecue sauce, just a little liquid hickory smoke. The name of this dish is a misnomer because there is no outdoor grill involved.

3 lb. large shrimp in shells, heads-on
2 sticks butter
10 cloves garlic, minced
2 tbsp. Worcestershire sauce
2 tbsp. freshly ground black pepper
¼ cup lemon juice, freshly squeezed
1 tsp. Tabasco
1 tsp. salt
½ tsp. cayenne pepper
½ cup white wine or beer
2 tsp. liquid hickory smoke

I almost never rinse shrimp, but in this case, I do because they go directly into the sauce. However, rinse them briefly and without washing any of the fat out of the heads. Drain well.

Preheat oven to 350 degrees. While shrimp are draining, place butter in a large baking pan or dish and melt in the oven. Meanwhile mince garlic and add to melting butter for a minute or two. Take pan out of oven, add all remaining ingredients, and mix well. Add shrimp and toss well.

Bake in oven for about 30 to 45 minutes, turning every 10 or 15 minutes. Time varies with size of shrimp. Shrimp are done when you can see them pulling away from the shells. Do not overcook. When you think they might be done, pull one out and taste it.

Serve shrimp in individual bowls with plenty of sauce and French bread for dipping.

Serves 6.

Corn and Shrimp Stew

The abundance of seafood in Louisiana inspired early French cooks to put shellfish into many vegetable dishes. Before pollution, or the knowledge of it, small river shrimp were highly prized and were a main ingredient to smothered corn and other vegetables. Corn and shrimp have paired off in so many ways that they are common partners. Try this as a little different twist. It can be eaten by itself or over rice.

1 lb. shrimp
6 ears fresh corn
2 tbsp. butter
1 tbsp. oil
2 tbsp. flour
1 large onion, chopped
1 bell pepper, chopped
2 cloves garlic, minced

3 cups shrimp stock (made from boiling shrimp peelings for 30 minutes)
2 cups tomatoes, fresh or canned, chopped
Salt, pepper, and Creole seasoning to taste

Peel shrimp and boil shells with 3½ cups water for 30 minutes.

Slice kernels of corn off cobs with a very sharp knife and scrape cobs with a dull knife. Set aside.

Heat butter and oil; add flour and cook, stirring constantly to make a blonde roux. Add chopped onion and bell pepper and sauté until soft. Add garlic and cook a minute more. Add stock, tomatoes, and seasonings, cover, and simmer for 10 minutes. Add corn and shrimp, cover, and simmer for 10 minutes.

Serves 4 to 6.

Shrimp Creole

Shrimp provides the largest seafood industry in the state, save menhaden, which is largely used for cat food and fish oil. And, Louisiana is the largest producer of shrimp in the country.

Two seasons produce brown shrimp from May to July and white shrimp from September to December, and the abundance keeps local prices down to a pittance, compared to the costs in northern markets.

There is virtually no limit to the use of shrimp in south Louisiana cooking. They star in appetizers, soups, gumbos, side dishes, and entrées. New dishes are created regularly, but the old ones are still around, too. One classic that has been popular for the better part of a century is shrimp Creole, which contains a well-seasoned, roux-based tomato gravy that is served over white rice. Its ingredients are local and its technique Creole to the core.

2 lb. shrimp
¼ cup flour
¼ cup vegetable oil
1 large onion, chopped
1 bell pepper, chopped
2 stalks celery, chopped
3 cloves garlic, minced
Juice of ½ lemon
1 8-oz. can tomato sauce

1 16-oz. can tomatoes (or substitute 6 large Creole tomatoes in season, peeled and chopped, for both tomato products)
Creole seasoning, salt, cayenne pepper, bay leaves, basil, and Worcestershire to taste
1 tbsp. sugar
2 tbsp. chopped parsley

Peel and devein shrimp and set aside in the refrigerator. Cover shrimp heads and shells in water, bring to a boil, cover, and simmer for 30 minutes for stock. Strain and set aside.

Make a roux with the flour and oil, stirring over medium heat until peanut butter-colored. Add chopped vegetables and sauté until soft. Add garlic and sauté a minute longer. Add lemon juice, tomatoes, seasonings, sugar, and about 1 cup of stock and simmer, covered, for about 30 minutes. Add shrimp and cook 10 minutes longer. Consistency should be slightly thick. Turn off fire and stir in parsley. Serve over white rice.

Serves 6 to 8.

Shrimp Po-Boy

The only place I know to get a good po-boy is in south Louisiana. The bread is better, and the cooks know how to fry seafood. Go north, east, or west and it's just not the same. A po-boy has to be made on New Orleans-style French bread. The texture is just right. Plus, we have the freshest shrimp, oysters, and soft-shell crabs, all of which make fantastic po-boys. Roast beef with gravy is pretty good, too. And, yes, the po-boy was another New Orleans invention. Bennie and Clovis Martin, on strike from streetcar conductor jobs, started selling sandwiches in the 1920s. They were nice enough to feed at no charge those "poor boys" who were also on strike and couldn't afford the cost of a meal. The meal: a slice of meat inside a length of French bread. The sandwich itself became known as a po-boy. When ordering a po-boy "dressed," a New Orleanian means "with lettuce and tomatoes." Preferred condiments are mayonnaise and butter. My favorite is oyster, but shrimp is high in popularity. The recipe below is the same for oysters, fish, or soft-shell crab. For a roast beef po-boy, do not use deli meat. Use leftovers from a home-cooked roast, thinly sliced, with plenty of gravy.

1 ½ lb. medium shrimp
1 egg
1 cup milk
2 cups vegetable oil
Corn flour (preferred), or a mixture of cornmeal and flour, about 2 cups

½ tsp. salt
¼ tsp. each black pepper and cayenne pepper
French bread, po-boy loaf
Mayonnaise
Lettuce, shredded
Tomatoes, sliced

Peel and devein shrimp.

Beat egg in a small bowl and whisk in milk.

Heat oil in narrow pot or deep fryer to 375 to 400 degrees. Heat oven to 450 degrees.

Place corn flour in a bowl and mix in seasonings. Dip each shrimp into eggwash and then corn flour. Shake off excess. Drop shrimp into hot oil individually and fry until golden brown (several minutes). Do not overcrowd pot.

Do not let temperature drop below 350 degrees, and try to keep it between 375 and 400. Continue frying until all are done. Drain on paper towels. Keep warm.

Cut loaf down the center and slather with mayonnaise. Place shrimp, then lettuce and tomatoes on bread and slice into fourths. Put sandwiches on a pan and place in the oven for about 1 minute or long enough to heat the bread only. Slice each sandwich in two and serve immediately. Serve with ketchup and hot sauce.

Serves 4.

Spinach-oyster Bake

Spinach and oysters make magnetic partners, and no pairing that I know of tastes better than this homey casserole. It's easy to put together and perfect for a pot luck.

3 dozen oysters

2 packages frozen chopped spinach

I 8-oz. package cream cheese, at room temperature

I stick butter, at room temperature

I large can artichokes, drained and sliced

Salt, pepper, and cayenne pepper

½ of I lemon

½ cup Italian breadcrumbs

¼ cup grated Parmesan cheese

I tbsp. butter

Drain oysters and check each one to remove any shell.

Cook spinach according to package directions and drain. In a large bowl, mix cream cheese and butter together. Stir in spinach and artichokes. Season to taste with salt, pepper, and cayenne pepper.

Place mixture into a 9-by-13-inch baking dish. Top with oysters. Squeeze lemon over oysters. Mix breadcrumbs and Parmesan cheese and sprinkle over oysters. Cut tbsp. of butter into small pieces and scatter on top of dish.

Bake in a 350-degree preheated oven until dish is bubbly and beginning to brown on top, about 15 minutes.

Serves 6 to 8.

Baked Oysters

An easy and delicious way to serve oysters is Italian style. That means breadcrumbs, garlic, olive oil, and flat-leaf parsley. This recipe can be baked in ramekins and served as a first course or in a baking dish for an entrée.

1 qt. oysters
1 tbsp. olive oil
6 green onions, chopped
2 cloves garlic, minced
1 tbsp. Italian seasoning
¼ tsp. each salt and pepper
Pinch cayenne pepper
1 tsp. lemon juice

1 cup seasoned Italian bread-
    crumbs plus some for topping
2 tbsp. chopped flat-leaf Italian
    parsley
2 tbsp. butter, cut into small
    pieces
3 tbsp. grated Parmesan cheese

Retaining the oyster liquid, place half the oysters one by one into the bottom of a 2-qt. casserole dish, removing any shell.

In the olive oil, sauté the green onions and garlic until soft and remove from heat. Add seasonings, lemon juice, breadcrumbs, and parsley. Place half of mixture on top of oysters and top with half the butter. Make another layer of the remaining oysters, checking for shell, and top with remaining crumb mixture. Pour ³/₄ cup of strained oyster liquid over the oysters. Sprinkle on top the cheese and remaining pieces of butter.

Bake in a preheated 350-degree oven for approximately 30 minutes, until oysters are curled and liquid absorbed. Let dish stand for about 10 minutes before serving.

Serves 4 as an entrée, 8 as an appetizer.

Oyster Pie

Louisiana is known for crawfish pies, but oyster eaters are sure to love this pie. The best oysters are in the winter, but you can get them year-round.

2 unbaked pastry shells, homemade (see index for recipe)
   or ready made, refrigerated
¼ cup vegetable oil
¼ cup flour
1 small onion, chopped
3 green onions, chopped
1 stalk celery, chopped
½ bell pepper, chopped
2 cloves garlic, minced
2 dozen large oysters or 3 dozen
   small and their water

½ tsp. salt
¼ tsp. freshly ground pepper
⅛ tsp. cayenne pepper
Dash Tabasco
Several dashes Worcestershire
   sauce
2 tbsp. minced parsley
¼ tsp. thyme leaves
4 oz. fresh mushrooms, sliced
3 tbsp. grated Parmesan cheese
3 slices bacon, cooked crisp and
   crumbled

Roll out pastry for a 9-inch pie plate. If using packaged refrigerated pastry, roll it thinner than it comes, about ⅛ inch thick. Place in pie plate. Set aside.

To make filling: Make a peanut butter-colored roux with the oil and flour. Add onions, celery, bell pepper, and garlic and cook on low heat until vegetables are soft.

Drain water from oysters. Add ½ cup of oyster water to roux. Add all seasonings and mushrooms and simmer for about 10 minutes. Add oysters and simmer until they curl, about 3 minutes. Pour into pie shell, sprinkle with cheese and bacon, and place a ⅛-inch-thick crust on top. Seal the edges and cut 3 slits in top crust for venting. Bake in a preheated 400-degree oven until brown, about 40 minutes. Let the pie sit for at least 15 minutes before serving.

Serves 4 to 6.

Alligator Sauce Piquant

Alligator as food is a novelty in Louisiana. When visitors come, they sometimes want to taste it. It's hard to find it in the stores, and I usually call around to seafood stores until I find some frozen. It's as easy to cook as chicken and, as they say, tastes something like chicken. To make it authentic Louisiana, try it in a sauce piquant, the Cajun's favorite spicy stew.

2 lb. alligator meat
I cup flour
I tsp. salt, divided
¾ tsp. cayenne pepper, divided
⅓ cup vegetable oil
I large onion, chopped
I bunch green onions, green and
   white parts divided, chopped
I bell pepper, chopped
2 stalks celery, chopped

3 cloves garlic, minced
I 14.5-oz. can diced Roma
   tomatoes
I 10-oz. can Rotel tomatoes
Freshly ground black pepper
½ tsp. thyme leaves
2 bay leaves
2½ cups water
I tsp. sugar
2 tbsp. chopped parsley leaves

Cut alligator meat into pieces, approximately 2-by-2 inches.

In a bowl, mix flour with ½ the salt and cayenne pepper. Heat oil in a large skillet. Dredge alligator pieces in the flour mixture, shake off excess, and brown well in the skillet, a few pieces at a time. Remove meat from the skillet and set aside. Sauté the onion, white part of the green onions, bell pepper, and celery in the oil, adding more if necessary, until transparent. Add the garlic and sauté a minute more. Add tomatoes, freshly ground pepper, thyme, bay leaves, remaining salt and cayenne pepper, water, and sugar and bring to a simmer. Add alligator meat and cook, covered, over low heat until alligator is tender, about 1 hour. Stir occasionally and adjust seasonings. (Sauce piquant should be spicy.) Add green onion tops and parsley in the last few minutes of cooking. Serve over rice.

Serves 6.

Seafood Lasagna

This is a dish for the make-ahead cook, the kind who doesn't like to cook after the guests arrive. You can actually make it the day before. Just remember that, if you are using a glass baking dish, take it out of the refrigerator at least 30 minutes before baking so that the dish won't break. I like to make it the same day simply because I think seafood should be served as fresh as possible, but that means making it in the morning, refrigerating it, and baking it in time for dinner that night. Seafood and pasta just go hand in hand, and a creamy white sauce brings it all together.

1½ lb. medium shrimp	½ cup grated Parmesan cheese
1 bag of seafood boiling spice	Salt and pepper to taste
1 lb. lump crabmeat, preferably jumbo	¼ tsp. garlic powder
	½ tsp. Creole seasoning
8 oz. lasagna noodles	15 oz. ricotta cheese
1 stick unsalted butter	1 cup finely chopped green onions
½ cup flour	1 cup shredded mozzarella
3 cups half-and-half	

Bring a large pot of water to a boil. Add 1 tsp. salt, shrimp, and a bag of seasonings and boil until just done, about 1 minute after coming back to a boil. Cool, peel, and devein. Pick through crabmeat to remove shell, being careful not to break it up too much. Boil lasagna noodles according to package directions, drain, rinse, and keep warm in pot with a little olive oil.

In a small saucepan, melt butter, remove from heat, and stir in flour. Gradually add half-and-half and stir to a smooth consistency. Put over medium heat and stir constantly until thickened and beginning to bubble around the edges. Do not boil. Remove from heat and add Parmesan cheese, salt, pepper, garlic powder, and Creole seasoning.

To assemble, spread ⅓ of the cream sauce on the bottom of a buttered 11-by-13-inch baking dish. Lay ⅓ of the noodles on top of the sauce. Layer the shrimp and cover with the ricotta cheese. Layer another ⅓ of noodles. Then sprinkle the crabmeat all over. Top with sauce and green onions. Add another layer of noodles, then sauce, and top with mozzarella. This can be held in the refrigerator, covered, until you are ready to serve. Remove from refrigerator at least 30 minutes before baking.

Preheat oven to 350 degrees. Bake for 30 minutes or until bubbling hot. Serves 8.

Crawfish Fettuccine

Whoever first mixed crawfish, cream sauce, and pasta together was a genius! And there is plenty of argument about who that was. Trademarked or not, chefs all over New Orleans keep their own good versions on the menus most of the time, and the Jazz Fest still sells tons of the trademarked one called Monica. All I know is that a Delgado Community College cooking instructor gave me this recipe years ago, and I am still using it.

2 cups half-and-half	Salt, pepper, and Creole seasoning
I cup heavy cream	to taste
6 green onions, chopped	Pinch cayenne pepper
2 cloves garlic, minced	I lb. fettuccine, preferably fresh
I stick butter	¾ cup freshly grated Parmesan
I lb. crawfish tails with fat	cheese, good quality

Combine half-and-half and cream in a small saucepan and reduce over medium-high heat for about 10 minutes, stirring occasionally. In a larger pot, sauté onions and garlic in butter until soft. Add crawfish, seasonings, and cream and reduce a little more until creamy.

While cream is reducing, cook pasta until al dente and drain. Place on a large platter and pour sauce over hot pasta. Add cheese and toss.

Serves 6.

Crawfish Étouffée

Until the legislature allocated funds for crawfish farming in 1959, crawfish were not marketed heavily in New Orleans. They were savored in bayou country as a wild catch during the January to June season. Early Creoles used crawfish sparingly in French-inspired dishes, but their recipes for *écrevisses* were a far cry from the heavy, spicy dishes that followed. Once New Orleanians caught on to their great flavor and versatility and to the fun of crawfish boils, rice farmers began alternating rice and crawfish crops to meet the demand.

Drawing once again from French influences, local cooks found that a stew, or étouffée, was the perfect foil for the tasty mudbug. Seasoned with cayenne pepper or hot sauce, Cajuns made it their own, serving it over fluffy white rice. With peeled crawfish tails abundant at the grocery stores, it is a simple dish to make, yet it holds its own at the fanciest of dinner parties. A medium-dark roux, frequently made with butter, and some of the crawfish fat make it rich and irresistible. To get the fat, buy Louisiana-packed peeled crawfish tails with fat. Alternatively, peel your own boiled crawfish tails and reserve the fat from the heads.

⅓ **cup flour**
5 **tbsp. butter, divided**
1 **onion, chopped**
½ **bell pepper, chopped**
2 **stalks celery, chopped**
3 **green onions, chopped, with white and green parts divided**
2 **cloves garlic, minced**
2 **tbsp. tomato paste**

1½ **cup seafood stock or bottled clam juice**
Salt, cayenne pepper, freshly ground black pepper, and Creole seasoning to taste
Worcestershire sauce
1 **lb. crawfish tails with fat**
2 **tbsp. chopped parsley**

Make a medium-dark roux of flour and 4 tbsp. of the butter. Add onion, bell pepper, celery, and white part of green onions and sauté for 10 minutes. Add garlic and sauté for 5 minutes more. Add tomato paste and cook for 5 minutes; then add stock, seasonings, Worcestershire, and crawfish, cover, and simmer for 15 minutes. In the last 5 minutes of cooking, add green onion tops. Remove from fire and stir in parsley and remaining tbsp. of butter. Serve over rice.

Serves 4.

Jambalaya

Jambalaya is one of the best combinations of Louisiana ingredients—rice from the land and seafood from the waters. Put them in a heavy pot with just the right touch of seasonings and an explosion of flavor is born.

A hallmark of Creole and Cajun cooking, jambalaya is believed to have gotten its name from the French word jambon meaning ham. From the beginning, Creole cooks relied heavily on pork, making the charcuterie an annual event of pig slaughtering where no single part of the pig went unused. Besides roasts, ribs, chops, sausage, and hams, many new products were forthcoming—hogshead cheese, pickled pigs' feet, and later, tasso, one of the strongest meat seasonings used in cooking today.

Jambalaya gets it share of pork, usually in the form of sausage and some- times tasso, pieces of slow wood-smoked pork shoulder. The great thing about the dish is that many ingredients can be used—or not. New Orleans cooks generally use tomato while Cajun cooks do not.

At its best, rice is seasoned with the holy trinity (onions, celery, and bell peppers) and simmers slowly in a spicy concoction of stock to which shrimp, sausage, and frequently chicken are added. It's an all-in-one affair that needs nothing more than crusty French bread and salad to become the perfect meal. Serve hot sauce on the side.

1 bag seafood boil
1½ lb. medium shrimp
¼ cup vegetable oil
1 chicken, cut into pieces
Salt, pepper, and cayenne pepper
1 onion, chopped
1 bell pepper, chopped
2 stalks celery, chopped
½ bunch green onions, chopped
3 cloves garlic, minced
4 cups reserved shrimp stock or
chicken stock or water
2 large Creole tomatoes, peeled
and chopped, or 18-oz. can
tomato sauce
½ lb. andouille sausage, sliced in ¼-
inch rounds
2 cups (1 lb.) rice
Salt, pepper, and Creole seasoning
to taste, about ½ tsp. each
2 tbsp. chopped parsley

Simmer a medium pot of water with bag of seasonings for about 15 minutes. Bring to a boil and add shrimp. Boil for 1 minute. Remove from fire and soak shrimp for 10 minutes. Strain and reserve liquid for stock. When cool, peel and devein shrimp. Set aside.

In a large, heavy pot, heat oil until hot. Season chicken pieces with salt and peppers and brown in oil on all sides. Remove pieces as browned and set aside. Add onion, bell pepper, celery, and green onions to pot and sauté over medium heat until soft. Add garlic and sauté another minute. Add stock or water and tomatoes and bring to a boil. Reduce to a simmer, return chicken to the pot, add sausage, and cook about 15 minutes. Add rice and seasonings, and simmer, covered, until rice has absorbed water, about 30 minutes. Stir once or twice during cooking. When done, gently stir in shrimp and parsley. Overstirring will make jambalaya mushy. Serve immediately, or reheat gently when ready to serve.

Serves 6.

Smothered Chicken

Before the surplus of fried chicken emporiums, people used to fry their own for Sunday dinners, but during the week, chicken was put into a gumbo or a skillet with onions and gravy. We called it smothered chicken, and sometimes stew or étouffée. Everyone agreed it was delicious, and it was a good way to stretch a chicken for a sizable family. The norm was to serve it over rice although it could be served with hot biscuits or grits. Here is a version enhanced by fresh mushrooms and wine.

1 whole chicken or your choice of pieces	1 large onion, chopped
1 ½ cups flour	2 stalks celery, chopped
2 tsp. salt	2 cloves garlic, minced
½ tsp. black pepper	½ cup water
¼ tsp. cayenne pepper	½ cup white wine
4 tbsp. vegetable oil	1 cup sliced fresh mushrooms
4 green onions, chopped, white and green parts divided	2 tbsp. chopped fresh flat-leafed parsley

Cut chicken into pieces, remove as much fat as possible, rinse well, and pat dry. Place flour in a large bowl and mix in seasonings. Heat oil in a large, heavy skillet. Dredge chicken pieces in flour, shake off excess, and brown well on all sides in medium-hot oil. You can do this in two batches. If oil dries up, add a little more. When well browned, cover chicken with white part of green onions, onion, celery, and garlic. Add water and wine and sprinkle with salt and pepper. Reduce heat to medium-low, cover skillet, and simmer for 1 hour, turning chicken and vegetables occasionally. Add mushrooms and simmer 15 minutes more or until chicken is very tender. Add green part of green onions and parsley in the last 5 minutes of cooking. Also at this point, taste for seasonings and add more if needed. Dip off any excess grease that accumulates on top. Serve over rice or with biscuits or grits.

Serves 4.

Drunken Chicken
(AKA BEER-CAN CHICKEN)

L eave it to Cajuns (and Texans, too, in this case) to find a different way to barbecue. What I like about this amazing recipe is that not only are the flavors divine, it is the easiest thing in the world to cook. Just sit those chickens on top of a few beer cans, close the barbecue grill, and forget about it. An hour and 20 minutes later, dinner is done.

1 whole chicken	**1 tsp. liquid crab boil**
Creole seasoning	**1 tsp. liquid smoke**
3 oz. beer	

Clean chicken and pat dry. Sprinkle inside and out with Creole seasoning. Light a charcoal grill and bring temperature to hot.

Meanwhile, pour a can of beer into a measuring cup. Measure 3 oz. and pour it back into the can. Add crab boil and liquid smoke.

When fire is hot, place chicken on top of beer can so that the chicken is sitting up with legs just touching the grill. The can is inside the cavity of chicken. Cover grill and cook for 1 hour and 20 minutes. Do not open grill during cooking. The result should be a very tasty chicken, moist on the inside and brown on the outside. Several chickens can be cooked like this at one time. Just line them in a row, each over its own beer can, over a hot fire. Cook the same amount of time, but don't open the grill. The heat and smoke must stay inside. It's OK to have one small vent open at the top or side of the grill.

Serves 2 to 4.

Option: A handful of wet hickory chips can be placed over the coals after they are hot.

Chicken Sauce Piquant

For some of us with a minimum of damage from Hurricane Katrina, cooking was the least that we could do after the storm. There were no restaurants, takeouts, or fast-food drive-throughs open so it was up to us to cook for ourselves and others who needed a place to go.

Welcome, the one-pot meal.

When feeding a crowd, nothing beats red beans, gumbo, vegetable soup, or chili. I got to looking back at some of the great-tasting, slow-cooking Creole/Cajun dishes that are relatively cheap to cook and revived my interest in some of the old ones such as sauce piquant. In the early days, this dish usually was made from a wild catch of rabbit, squirrel, alligator, turtle, frogs, or armadillo. Today's cook might choose beef or chicken unless a hunter in the family brings home more exotic fare.

Sauce piquant (pee-KHAW) is nothing more than a roux-based stew with tomatoes and meat, fowl, or seafood. It allows you to use an inexpensive or less tender cut of meat because the slow cooking melts away the toughness. The basic ingredients begin with the trinity—onions, bell peppers, celery— that we all know so well, but what characterizes sauce piquant from a stew in Kansas or a fricassee in Oregon is the spiciness from cayenne pepper and added flavor from lots of trinity plus garlic. Gourmet cooks may add a splash of wine, and rice or noodles go well on the side. But the name itself— piquant, meaning hot, spicy, or pungent in French—dictates that some form of hot peppers are used. Sometimes it is confused with picante sauce, a condiment that can be served with meats, but it is not a sauce in which meat is cooked.

If you didn't grow up in south Louisiana, you may have never heard of sauce piquant. The dish is unique to the local culture and rarely found on a restaurant menu. More Cajun than Creole, it originally utilized ingredients obtainable from the land by the poorest of people. Yet their imagination and cooking skills elevated it to heights fit for a party. Chicken is the easiest choice of meat, but feel free to substitute alligator, rabbit, or turtle.

½ cup vegetable oil
Flour
Salt, black pepper, and cayenne
   pepper
10 to 12 chicken thighs or a combination of legs and thighs or 1
   whole chicken, cut into pieces
   (about 5 lb.)*
1 large onion, chopped
1 bunch green onions, chopped,
   white and green parts divided
1 bell pepper, chopped

2 ribs celery, chopped
3 cloves garlic, minced
2 8-oz. cans tomato sauce
1 14-oz. can chicken stock
½ cup red wine
1 tsp. thyme leaves
3 bay leaves
Creole seasoning
2 splashes Tabasco sauce
1 tbsp. Worcestershire sauce
2 tbsp. chopped flat-leaf parsley

Heat oil in a large, heavy pot. Place about 1 cup of flour in a bowl and season heavily with salt and peppers, about ½ tsp. each. Dredge chicken pieces in flour and keep unused seasoned flour for use in roux. Brown chicken in medium-hot oil until well browned on each side. Remove chicken to plate.

Pour oil from skillet into measuring cup, leaving all browned particles in the bottom of the pot to enhance the sauce. Add oil to cup if necessary to make ½ cup and return oil to pot. Heat oil to medium and add ½ cup of reserved seasoned flour, stirring to mix well. Continue stirring to make a dark brown roux. When roux is desired color, add onions, white parts of green onions, bell peppers, and celery and sauté over medium heat until vegetables are limp, about 5 minutes. Add garlic and sauté a couple of minutes more. Stir in tomato sauce until smooth and add chicken stock and wine. Bring to a simmer and add thyme, bay leaves, Creole seasoning, Tabasco, and Worcestershire. Simmer for a few minutes and taste. Adjust seasonings, particularly salt and cayenne pepper. A true sauce piquant is spicy so add plenty of cayenne. Return chicken to the pot, keeping heat at a simmer, cover pot, and cook for 1 hour, stirring occasionally. Remove bay leaves. When done, add green onion tops and parsley. Serve with rice or noodles.

Serves 6.

*Domestic rabbit or wild game such as alligator can be substituted for chicken. If using deboned alligator meat, use about 2 lb. and cut into 1-inch cubes.

Chicken and Dumplings

I always thought my mother made the best biscuits I ever ate, and for years, I tried to duplicate them. I would watch her and write down everything step-by-step, but since she didn't measure anything, my estimates never stood up to the task. She used the same dough for dumplings, simply rolling it a bit thinner than for biscuits. Instead of rounds, she cut them into little rectangles that puffed up perfectly in the chicken stock. She used a wide pot and put in as many dumplings as would cover the top tightly. Here again, my efforts never quite matched up until one day, I got a bright idea. Somewhere, through friends, we had discovered frozen biscuits made and marketed locally. They were almost—very close—as good as my mother's. Why couldn't I use them for dumplings? This was before mini frozen biscuits so I took the large ones, cut them in fourths and dropped them into the simmering pot of chicken. Bingo! It worked. Call it the sign of modern times, but now, when I make chicken and dumplings, I spare myself the mess of flouring a kitchen counter and rolling out dough and simply pull some frozen biscuits out of my freezer and save about 30 minutes.

I whole chicken
2 large onions
4 stalks celery
3 tbsp. butter
½ tsp. celery salt
I tsp. salt
½ tsp. black pepper

¼ tsp. cayenne pepper
¼ teaspoon dried thyme leaves
3 bay leaves
½ cup flour
I cup milk
6 large frozen biscuits*

Rinse chicken, saving liver for another use. In a large pot, cover chicken and remaining giblets with water and bring to a boil. Add 1 onion, quartered, and 2 stalks celery, cut into chunks. Cover and reduce heat and simmer until tender, about 40 minutes. Remove chicken and giblets to a plate and continue cooking stock, uncovered, to reduce a little, about 15 minutes. When cool enough, strain and reserve stock.

Debone chicken and shred or cut meat into bite-size pieces. Chop the remaining onion and 2 stalks celery.

In the same pot, melt butter and sauté onions and celery. When vegetables are wilted, add stock and seasonings. Simmer for 15 minutes. Meanwhile, whisk flour into milk until smooth. Add milk and chicken to pot and simmer to thicken for about 10 minutes.

About an hour before serving, take biscuits out of freezer to thaw partially. About 30 minutes before serving, heat chicken mixture to hot but not boiling. Cut each biscuit into four pieces and drop pieces into pot. Cover, reduce heat, and simmer until dumplings are cooked, about 10 to 15 minutes. Dumplings should be puffed up and tender.

Serve in soup bowls with extra biscuits on the side.

Serves 6.

*Or make homemade buttermilk biscuits from scratch. (See index for recipe.)

Panéed Veal

The Italian influence in Creole cooking is major. In fact, so many of the neighborhood restaurants throughout the New Orleans area tout two things—Italian food and seafood. On the Italian side of the menus are dishes like stuffed artichokes, eggplant parmigiana, and lots of veal. Panéed veal has always been a local favorite and a simple dish for home cooks. In other places, it might be called a breaded veal cutlet. The ultimate, of course, is white baby veal pounded thin, but calf cut into scallops and pounded thin will work quite well.

1½ lb. veal round or cutlets, baby or calf	¼ cup olive oil
Salt and freshly ground black pepper	Lemon wedges
	Parmesan cheese
2 eggs, beaten	Parsley, minced
½ cup milk	½ cup white wine, broth, or water
2 cups breadcrumbs, Italian seasoned	

Pound veal with mallet on waxed paper until thin, about ¼ inch thick. Some cuts of baby veal cutlets are already thin enough and do not require pounding. If cutlets are large, cut into pieces about 4-by-3 inches. Sprinkle with salt and pepper.

Mix eggs and milk in a bowl, and place breadcrumbs on a sheet of waxed paper.

In a large, heavy skillet, heat oil to hot. Dip veal scallops into egg wash, let it drip off, and dredge them through breadcrumbs. Put into hot skillet and brown for about 1 minute on each side. Take up briefly on paper towels and place on a platter. Squeeze lemon over veal, sprinkle lightly with Parmesan and then with parsley. Pour oil from pan and deglaze pan with ½ cup white wine, broth, or water. Pour this over veal and serve immediately.

Serves 6.

Veal Chops with Mushrooms and Marsala

Veal has long been a Creole favorite, often preferred over beef. Veal chops make a quick yet gourmet meal ideal for weeknight dinners. Keeping a bottle of Marsala on tap is a key to dressing up easy meals.

4 veal chops, ½ to ¾ inch thick
Salt, freshly ground pepper, and
   Creole seasoning to taste
1 tbsp. butter
1 tbsp. olive oil

3 green onions, chopped fine
1 clove garlic, minced
1 cup sliced mushrooms
¼ cup Marsala

Sprinkle veal chops lightly with seasonings. Heat butter and olive oil in a large skillet until hot. Sear veal chops for about 2 minutes on each side and remove chops to a plate. Sauté onions and garlic in skillet for about 2 minutes, add mushrooms and sauté 2 minutes more. Taste and add salt, freshly ground pepper, and Creole seasoning to taste. Stir in Marsala and cook for 2 minutes more. Return chops to skillet, heat through, and serve.

To make this in advance, let the mushroom sauce and veal chops cool. When ready to serve, heat sauce, add chops, and heat. Do not overcook.

Serves 4.

Grillades

Grillades is the quintessential Creole brunch dish dating as far back as the mid-nineteenth century when Mesdames Begue and Esparbe prepared them for riverfront market workers. An early lunch, or brunch, fueled the butchers, fishermen, and farmers who had worked since daybreak and were in need of something rib-sticking. Grillades and grits filled the bill in those little cafés that became some of the city's first restaurants.

The dish is a natural for brunches, Saints parties, and Carnival buffets served with king cake, bread pudding, or bananas Foster. Grillades is a New Orleans creation. It is not only served to kings of Carnival. It was a favorite dish among the poorer classes of Creoles, served at breakfast and dinner. To make grillades, pound a round steak, beef or veal, until thin, cut it into squares or strips, and lightly brown it in hot oil. Versions range from briefly cooking tender baby veal, a restaurant preference, to the long, slow simmering of the tougher beef round.

2 lb. veal or beef round steak,
    about ½ inch thick
Salt, pepper, and Creole seasoning
2 tbsp. plus ½ cup vegetable oil
½ cup flour
1 large onion, chopped
1 bell pepper, chopped
2 stalks celery, chopped
1 bunch green onions, chopped with
    white and green parts divided
3 large cloves garlic, minced
1 14.5-oz. can diced tomatoes, or

3 large Creole tomatoes, peeled
    and diced, when in season
2 cups water
½ cup red wine
Salt, freshly ground pepper, and
    Creole seasoning to taste
2 bay leaves
½ tsp. thyme
Few dashes Tabasco
1 tbsp. Worcestershire sauce
¼ cup chopped fresh flat-leafed
    parsley

Trim round steak of fat and bone and rub with seasonings. Pound to ¼ inch thickness and cut into pieces about 2-by-3 inches.

Heat 2 tbsp. oil in a large, heavy pot. Brown meat pieces on both sides a few at a time being careful not to overcrowd pot. Set meat aside. (Brown bits in bottom of pot will be absorbed as other ingredients are added.)

Add ½ cup of oil to pot and stir in flour to make a roux. Stir constantly over medium heat until roux is dark brown but not burned. Immediately add onion, bell pepper, celery, and white part of green onions. Reduce heat and cook for a few minutes, stirring. Add garlic, cook for another minute, and stir in tomatoes, water, and wine. Add remainder of ingredients except green onion tops and parsley. Stir well and return meat to pot. Simmer, covered, until meat is fork tender, about 1½ to 2 hours, stirring occasionally. When finished, add ¼ cup green onion tops and parsley. Serve over grits or grits soufflé (see index for Grits Soufflé).

Serves 6.

Shortcuts: Instead of chopping onions, bell pepper, celery, garlic, and parsley, substitute 2 14-oz. containers of fresh-cut Creole seasoning mix. Buy deboned and trimmed round steaks.

Creole Daube

Daube is one of the great winter meals in New Orleans though it sits high on the list of endangered or lost dishes, i.e. those rarely cooked by the young folks and fading from the menus of neighborhood restaurants. Yet it remains a wonderful example of how French and Italian cooking merge in this food mecca, be it in restaurants or at home.

In its classic French form, daube (pronounced dohb) is a beef roast that is larded or stuffed with salt pork slivers and cooked in broth and wine until tender. It becomes daube glacé with the addition of gelatin and is classy party fare sliced thin and served with crackers, a hoity-toity cousin to hogshead cheese. But the home-style, what's-for-dinner daube can be as simple as a beef roast cooked in red gravy until falling apart and served with spaghetti.

Beef daube, sometimes called Italian daube, is a marriage of French and Italian cuisine that begins with the French style of braising beef with red wine, vegetables, and herbs. This is where you stop if daube glacé is your final goal, adding gelatin and chilling for the exquisite buffet. The Italian forces come in with the red gravy, known elsewhere as spaghetti sauce, with or without a roux base, and pasta. Some recipes call for cooking the daube in wine and stock and preparing the red gravy separately. For simplicity in today's rushed lifestyle, it is mandatory for most cooks to cook it all together in one big pot. A good name for the resulting hearty dish is, simply, Creole daube.

Various cuts of beef suit daube, including the rump, round, shoulder, or chuck. Instead of larding, a no-no in contemporary consumption, a stuffing of garlic proves equally flavorful. Old Creole recipes used lard for the braising, too, but olive oil substitutes healthfully and tastefully. Don't be put off by the long, slow-cooking process. The dish can simmer on the stove with little attention while you catch up on rest and relaxation.

1 3-lb. rump roast
5 cloves garlic, 2 slivered and 3 minced
Salt, pepper, and Creole seasoning
2 tbsp. olive oil
1 large onion, chopped
1 bell pepper, chopped
2 ribs celery, chopped
1 6-oz. can tomato paste
1 8-oz. can tomato sauce
1 cup red wine
1 14-oz. can beef broth
1 tbsp. Italian seasoning
¼ to ½ tsp. cayenne to taste, additional salt if needed, and a pinch of sugar
2 tbsp. chopped fresh flat-leaf parsley

With a sharp knife or ice pick, punch holes in the roast about 2 inches apart and stuff with slivers of garlic. Rub roast generously with salt, pepper, and Creole seasoning. Heat oil in a heavy pot or Dutch oven and brown roast well on all sides over medium-high heat. When browned, take roast out of pot and set aside.

In the same oil, sauté onion, bell pepper, and celery over medium heat until soft, about 10 minutes, stirring occasionally. Add minced garlic and cook for 5 more minutes. Add tomato paste and cook, stirring frequently, almost until it begins to brown, about 10 minutes. Add tomato sauce and cook over medium heat, stirring occasionally, for 5 more minutes. Add wine, beef broth, Italian seasoning, cayenne, salt if needed, and sugar and stir well. Return roast to pot fat side up, turn fire to low, cover, and simmer for 4 hours or until roast is very tender. Stir well every hour and turn roast over halfway through cooking. Sprinkle with parsley and serve with spaghetti.

Serves 6.

Shortcut: Instead of making the red gravy, you can substitute your favorite spaghetti sauce. In this case, leave out the tomato paste, tomato sauce, onion, bell pepper, celery, and minced garlic, and add a 26-oz. jar of prepared sauce when you add the wine and broth. Sauce may be slightly thinner using prepared sauce and can be reduced by uncovering the pot for the last ½ hour of cooking.

Pot Roast with Vegetables

There is no better friend to the family cook than a pot roast. You can cook meat, vegetables, and gravy all in one pot for dinner; then warm up the beef and gravy the next night for po-boys. A pot roast basically cooks itself while you do something else. Stuff it with garlic for maximum flavor.

3 large cloves garlic
1 3- to 4-lb. rump roast
Salt, pepper, and Creole seasoning
2 tsp. vegetable oil
1 large onion, chopped

¼ cup Worcestershire sauce
1 cup water
3 medium russet potatoes
3 carrots
2 tbsp. flour

Peel garlic and cut into thin strips. Pierce roast with a sharp knife or ice pick and stuff with garlic strips. Cuts should be 2 to 3 inches apart and deep enough to conceal garlic. Press meat back together after garlic is inserted.

Sprinkle roast liberally on all sides with salt, pepper, and Creole seasoning.

In a large heavy pot, heat oil to medium-high and brown roast on all sides. Do not burn, but let the meat brown well. Place onions on top of roast. Pour Worcestershire sauce over onions. Cover pot, reduce heat, and simmer roast for about 1 hour. Turn roast over. If liquids from the roast tend to dry up, add about ½ cup water. Peel potatoes, cut in half or thirds and place around the roast. Scrape carrots, cut in thirds and place in pot with potatoes. Sprinkle vegetables with salt, pepper, and Creole seasoning. Simmer, covered, for another hour, turning vegetables after 30 minutes.

When roast is tender and vegetables done, remove them from pot. You should have a cup or so of liquid remaining in the pot.

In a small bowl or cup, stir flour into the ½ cup of water until there are no lumps remaining. This should be done gradually so that flour is smooth after a small amount of water has been added. Gradually pour the mixture through a strainer into the pot, stirring constantly. Heat over medium heat until gravy has thickened. If too thick, add a little more water until a good consistency is reached. When gravy is complete, return roast and vegetables to pot, heating when ready to serve.

To serve, cut roast across the grain. Slice about ¼ inch thick and serve on a platter surrounded by vegetables. Spoon a little gravy over the meat and vegetables and serve the rest on the side.

Serves 6 to 8.

Creole Meat Loaf

Creoles were great lovers of veal and pork. Unlike most American meat loaves that are made of beef only, a New Orleans-style meat loaf is likely to be composed of all three meats. They are even packaged together in a two-pound trio in most of the city's grocery stores. Green onions and parsley are mandatory as well as some Creole seasoning. If you're worried that pork makes the meat loaf too fatty, just pour off the grease if it accumulates. The fat is removed yet the flavor remains.

1 2-lb. meat loaf package of ground beef, veal, and pork	1 6-oz. can tomato paste, divided
1 bunch green onions, chopped	½ cup Italian-seasoned bread-crumbs
½ bell pepper, chopped	½ tsp. salt
3 cloves garlic, minced	¼ tsp. freshly ground black pepper
1 tbsp. vegetable oil	½ tsp. Creole seasoning
2 eggs, beaten	

Place meat in a large bowl.

Sauté onions, bell pepper, and garlic in oil until soft. Add to bowl of meat along with eggs, 1 tbsp. of the tomato paste, breadcrumbs, and seasonings. Mix well and form into loaf. Bake this in a loaf pan, or shape into a loaf and place loaf in the center of a large baking pan. With either type of pan, grease can be poured or spooned off during and after cooking. Bake in a preheated 350-degree oven for about 1 hour or until meat loaf is browning. Top with remaining tomato paste mixed with 2 tbsp. water, sprinkle with salt, pepper, and Creole seasoning and bake at 400 degrees for 15 minutes or until the top is browning again.

Leftovers make great sandwiches, served cold with mayonnaise.

Serves 6 to 8.

Standing Rib Roast

My choice for Christmas dinner is a standing rib roast. So close to Thanksgiving when turkey is king, Christmas demands something of its own. And unlike the multiple trimmings that go with the turkey, a rib roast mercifully requires only potatoes au gratin and a fresh green vegetable.

Choosing your roast is of major importance. There are thirteen ribs to a side of beef and seven make up the rib cut. The sixth through the twelfth ribs are the tenderest so you may want to consult your butcher to make sure you are getting the best ribs. Also ask him to remove the chine bone. When slicing the cooked roast, you may want to remove the ribs by cutting the meat away as close as possible. This makes it much easier to slice.

1 5- to 7-rib beef roast	Garlic powder
Coarse sea salt	Horseradish Sauce
Freshly ground black pepper	

About 1 hour before cooking, sprinkle the roast liberally with coarse sea salt, freshly cracked black pepper, and garlic powder. Preheat oven to 450 degrees. Insert meat thermometer into center of roast away from bones. Place roast fat side up on a rack in a shallow pan.

Sear the roast in the oven for about 25 minutes and reduce heat to 325. Roast until thermometer reaches the temperature you choose. Timing should be approximately 15 minutes per lb. for rare, 18 to 20 per lb. for medium, and 25 minutes per lb. for well done.

Let finished roast sit at room temperature for 20 minutes before carving to allow the juices to coagulate. Skim off the fat from the meat drippings and use remaining juices as au jus. Serve with fresh horseradish sauce.

Serves 6 to 8.

Horseradish Sauce: Mix together 1 part fresh horseradish (available in the refrigerated section of grocery store) to 1 part mayonnaise and 2 parts sour cream. Season to taste with salt and freshly ground black pepper.

7 Steaks in Gravy

Gravy steaks may be poor man's food, but in the '50s, it was what you wanted for dinner. There was nothing better than a pot of bone-in 7 steaks with plenty of gravy to be served over rice or grits. Some green peas or other vegetable on the side and some hot biscuits or cornbread added up to a feast fit for a king. Sadly, it's hard to find bone-in gravy steaks any more. Most cuts of less expensive beef are sold boneless, but the bones imparted much of the flavor in dishes such as this. These steaks get their name from the shape of their bones, which looks like a 7. Ask your butcher for bone-in (maybe he'll take the hint and order some), but if you can't find them, the boneless will do. These steaks are also used for 7-steak gumbo and can make a good pot of grillades if you cook it long enough for the meat to become tender.

2 lb. bone-in 7 steaks, or 1 to 1 ½ lb. boneless	4 green onions, chopped with white and green divided
4 tbsp. vegetable oil, divided	3 cloves garlic, minced
Salt, pepper, and Creole seasoning	1 cup water
½ cup flour	1 bay leaf
1 bell pepper, chopped	Pinch thyme leaves
1 medium onion, chopped	Dash Worcestershire sauce
1 stalk celery, chopped	4 sprigs parsley, chopped

If steaks are large, cut them into pieces about 3-by-3 inches. Heat 3 tbsp. of the oil in a medium pot or large skillet. Stir a liberal amount of salt, pepper, and Creole seasoning into flour. Dredge steaks in flour and brown over medium-high heat on both sides. Remove steaks from skillet and set aside.

Add remaining tbsp. of oil to skillet. Sauté bell pepper, onion, celery, and white parts of green onions in oil until transparent. Add garlic and sauté a minute or two more. Stir in water and add bay leaf, thyme, and Worcestershire, along with salt, pepper and Creole seasoning to taste. When mixture is hot, return steaks to skillet. Lower heat to a simmer and place top on skillet. Cook for 2 hours over low heat, stirring occasionally. If mixture thickens too much, add ¼ cup water. About 5 minutes before done, add green onion tops and parsley.

Serves 4.

Boiled Beef

Tujague's, one of the oldest restaurants in New Orleans, is famous for its boiled beef brisket. A simple dish, it is served with a sauce of horseradish, ketchup, and Creole mustard. The Creoles used many versions of boiled beef including the bouilli, or leftover soup meat. Later, restaurants used the beef brisket to complete the dish, although any cuts of beef can be used. Because the brisket has a high fat content, a leaner cut can be substituted when calories are a concern.

1 tbsp. canola oil	6 cloves garlic, peeled
1 3- to 4-lb. beef brisket, rump, round, or sirloin roast, excess fat removed	3 bay leaves
	1 tbsp. whole peppercorns
	1 tbsp. salt
1 large onion, quartered	1 tbsp. Worcestershire sauce
3 stalks celery, halved	

Heat oil to hot in a heavy Dutch oven. Brown roast on all sides. Add water almost to cover roast and add all other ingredients. Bring to a boil and reduce heat to a simmer. Cover and cook for 2½ hours. The meat should be very tender. Serve with horseradish sauce (see index for Horseradish Sauce).
Serves 4.

Note: You can strain stock and use for soup or another dish. Or, for side vegetables to go with the boiled beef, add large chunks of carrots and potatoes in the last ½ hour of cooking.

Brisket Stuffed with Crawfish Dressing

One of my favorite things to take to a Carnival parade party is a brisket. For one thing, it feeds a lot of people. Plus, everyone seems to love it. Stuff one with a crawfish dressing, and it serves more and tastes even better.

1 beef brisket, 6 to 8 lb., trimmed of most fat but not all
A mixture of 1 tbsp. salt, 1 tbsp. Creole seasoning, 1 tsp. pepper, 1 tsp. cayenne pepper, and 1 tsp. garlic powder, divided
2 medium onions, divided
½ bell pepper
1 stalk celery

4 green onions
1 lb. crawfish tails, coarsely chopped*
4 or 5 cloves garlic, minced
2 tbsp. chopped fine parsley
1 cup breadcrumbs, Italian seasoned
1 egg
¼ cup Worcestershire sauce

With a sharp knife, cut a pocket into the brisket horizontally so that the edges of uncut meat run at least 1 inch on all three sides. Be sure not to puncture the meat on top or bottom. Using 1 tbsp. of the mixed dried seasoning, sprinkle meat inside and out.

In a food processor, chop 1 onion until almost mushy. Set aside. Chop remaining onion, bell pepper, celery, and green onions until fine and almost shredded. Mix with crawfish tails, garlic, parsley, breadcrumbs, egg, and the other tbsp. of seasoning, and stuff into pocket. Close the pocket by sewing it together with cotton kitchen string or linen twine, using a large needle (tapestry needle). Make stitches fairly close together, about ½ inch.

Place brisket in a large baking pan. Sprinkle top with Worcestershire and the remaining cup of onions. Tightly enclose the top of the baking pan with heavy tin foil and bake at 275 degrees for 4 hours. Check every hour or so to see if the pan is drying out. If so, add about a ½ cup of water. (Brisket will probably release a lot of juices. You can pour these off into a bowl, set it in the freezer and remove fat from top.) After 4 hours, remove foil, raise temperature to 325 degrees and cook for 1 more hour. When done, let the brisket set for at least 20 minutes before serving. You can deglaze the pan with a little water on top of the stove, add defatted juices and pour over the brisket. Or, serve as gravy on the side. Thicken the gravy, if you wish, with flour or cornstarch. To serve, slice brisket across the grain.

Serves 8 to 10.

*Most packaged frozen crawfish tails are now portioned in 12 oz. You can either use one of these and reduce other ingredients slightly, including size of brisket, or, buy 2 and cut a 4-oz. portion off one by defrosting slightly and returning the rest to the freezer.

Spaghetti and Meatballs

Speaking the language in New Orleans means understanding that a street's grassy median is a neutral ground and that the red stuff that goes on pasta is red gravy. Some cooks even put a roux under what others call a marinara sauce. In south Louisiana, this gravy is more potent, heavier, and almost meaty when there's no meat in it. The meat is, of course, in the meatballs. They are potent, too. Lots of garlic and seasonings make them just right. Some of the Sicilian descendants like to brown the tomato before getting started because it gives the gravy a darker color right off the bat. Then, some cheese is added to the gravy as well as to the meatballs. Instead of seasoned breadcrumbs from a can, torn French or Italian bread is preferred. Mama mia! This is old school and delicious.

MEATBALLS:
- 1 lb. ground beef or veal
- 1 lb. lean ground pork
- 3 1-inch-thick slices French bread
- 2 eggs, beaten
- 1 small onion
- 1 green onion
- 1 stalk celery
- ¼ bell pepper
- 3 cloves garlic
- ⅓ cup grated Parmesan cheese
- ½ tsp. salt
- ½ tsp. Creole seasoning
- ¼ tsp. freshly ground pepper
- 1 tbsp. minced fresh parsley leaves
- 1 tsp. dried oregano
- 2 tbsp. olive oil

SAUCE:
3 tbsp. olive oil, divided
3 6-oz. cans tomato paste
1 15-oz. can tomato sauce
1 large onion, chopped
3 green onions, chopped with
    white and green parts divided
2 stalks celery, chopped
1 bell pepper, chopped
3 large cloves garlic, minced
4 cups water
½ cup red wine
2 bay leaves

1 tsp. oregano
1 tsp. Italian seasoning
1½ tsp. salt
1 tsp. Creole seasoning
1 tsp. freshly ground black pepper
1 tsp. sugar
⅓ cup grated Parmesan cheese
2 tbsp. chopped parsley leaves

PASTA:
1 tsp. salt
Few drops olive oil
1 lb. spaghetti or thin spaghetti

To make meatballs: Mix ground meats in a large bowl. Cut or tear bread into small pieces. In a small bowl, soak bread in beaten eggs. Chop onions, celery, and bell pepper into large chunks and pulse in a food processor until chopped fine. Crush garlic in a press and add vegetables to meat. Add cheese, salt, Creole seasoning, pepper, parsley, and oregano. Finally, add soaked bread. Mix well with hands and form into meatballs about 2 inches in diameter. You should have about 40. Heat olive oil in large, heavy skillet and brown meatballs well on all sides over medium-high heat. Brown in 2 or 3 batches. Turn frequently with a metal spatula to keep meatballs from sticking. Add extra oil if needed. When browned, remove meatballs from skillet and drain on paper towels. Set aside. Reserve skillet with all the brown drippings.

To make sauce: Lightly oil a large heavy pot with 1 tbsp. of olive oil. Add tomato paste and sauce and cook over medium-high heat, stirring often, until almost browning. A silicon spatula works well for stirring this. Be careful not to burn. When slightly darkened, remove from heat and set aside. This will take about 20 minutes.

In the skillet used for meatballs, add 2 tbsp. olive oil if needed. You may have oil left from browning the meatballs. Sauté the onion, white part of green onions, celery, and bell pepper until transparent. Add garlic and sauté a minute more. Add this mixture to the tomato sauce along with water, wine, seasonings, and sugar. Mix well, cover, and simmer for 30 minutes. Stir occasionally. Add meatballs, cheese, parsley, and green onion tops and simmer for 30 minutes more.

When almost ready to serve, heat a pot of boiling water. Add salt and oil. Add pasta, stirring vigorously, and boil until al dente, about 10 minutes for spaghetti, 5 for thin spaghetti. Drain in a colander. Serve with sauce and meatballs. Pass freshly grated Parmesan or, better yet, a wedge of good Parmesan with a small grater at the table.

Serves 6 to 8.

Boudin

Residents of Cajun country, or south Louisiana near Lafayette, eat as well as New Orleanians. Some preferences are different. For example, city folks use tomatoes in gumbo and jambalaya and Cajuns do not. And then there's boudin, a Cajun rice sausage made with pork and liver. In New Orleans, you can buy boudin in the grocery stores, and chefs put it on menus in creative ways. But in the country, it's a staple often eaten for breakfast and most often purchased at convenience stores, such as those at filling stations. You'll find it hot in crock pots or other electrical servers, and you'll start eating it as you walk out of the store. Cajuns are great cooks, and they invented boudin as a way to use every part of the hog at slaughtering time. Because rice was the major crop, they took the intestines and filled them with liver, rice, seasonings, and spice. They could cook and eat it on the spot, at the great party known as the boucherie, where pork was divided up and preserved for months to come. It's hard to find pork liver in grocery stores, but you can substitute chicken livers. Boudin is much like dirty rice. I like it because you can use it as a stuffing for Cornish hens and chickens. Or, just have a link with a cold beer.

2 lb. pork butt, cut into 1-inch
 cubes
¾ lb. pork liver, cut into 1-inch
 cubes, or chicken livers
1 onion, chopped
2 bunches green onions, chopped,
 divided
2 celery stalks, chopped
4 cloves garlic, chopped
8 cups water
4 tsp. salt, divided
2 tsp. black pepper, divided
2 tsp. cayenne pepper, divided
6 cups cooked white rice
1 cup finely chopped parsley

In a large pot, cover meat, onion, 1 bunch of the green onions, celery, and garlic with water. Add 1 tsp. each of the salt, black pepper, and cayenne pepper and bring to a boil. Reduce heat and simmer until the meat is tender, about 1 hour and 45 minutes.

Remove pot from heat and strain, reserving liquid. Let the mixture cool slightly and put ingredients through a meat grinder set on coarse grind. Or, chop finely with a heavy knife.

Place the ground meat in a large bowl. Mix in the cooked rice, remaining green onions, parsley, remaining 3 tsp. salt and 1 tsp. each of black and cayenne peppers, and 1 cup of reserved cooking liquid and stir well. If mixture is too dry, add more broth to make a moist dressinglike consistency. Cool to room temperature or overnight in the refrigerator.

Using a sausage stuffer or funnel, stuff the sausage into rinsed natural casings, making links of about 4 to 6 inches, twisting between each link. You will need about 6 feet of casings. When ready to eat, poach the links gently in water for about 10 minutes. Cooking in a microwave, on a grill, or frying, may cause the sausages to split. The sausage may be removed from casings and used for stuffing poultry for baking or making boudin balls by dredging spoonfuls in egg wash, rolling in breadcrumbs, and frying in hot oil.

Makes 4 pounds of sausage.

Pork Chops and Noodles

Everyone loves this dish. I have no idea of the origin of it, but my mother made it as far back as I can remember. It is great served with a salad on the side.

4 tbsp. vegetable oil	½ bell pepper, chopped
Salt and pepper	I rib celery, chopped
6 center-cut pork chops, ½ inch thick	I 15-oz. can tomatoes
	¼ tsp. cayenne pepper
I cup flour	I 12-oz. package egg noodles
I medium onion, chopped	¾ cup grated cheddar cheese

In a skillet, heat oil. Salt and pepper pork chops and roll in flour. Brown pork chops on both sides. Remove from skillet and place on dish.

To the oil, add chopped vegetables and sauté. Add tomatoes and cook a little longer. Add about 2 cups of water and put pork chops back into mixture. Salt and pepper to taste and add cayenne pepper. Lower heat, cover, and simmer for about 45 minutes, stirring a couple of times to keep from sticking.

While this cooks, cook noodles until just done in boiling salted water. Drain. Place drained noodles in an 11-by-13-inch baking dish. Mix in tomato mixture and place pork chops on top. Sprinkle cheese on top. Bake in a preheated 350-degree oven for 30 to 45 minutes until bubbly and slightly browned on top.

Serves 6.

Pasta Milanese

Nowhere outside of Italy is the observance of St. Joseph's Day more pronounced than in New Orleans.

It all started during a famine in Sicily when the residents prayed to St. Joseph, the earthly father of Jesus, to intercede. Soon crops grew plentifully, and the patron saint was honored with the most precious possession—food. Altars of bread, fish, artichokes, pastries, and other delicacies were and still are built to thank St. Joseph for favors such as prosperity and healing.

Many Sicilians migrated to the New Orleans area in the nineteenth and twentieth centuries, forming one of the largest concentrations of Italians in America. Their culinary traditions continue to influence home cooking as well as the restaurant scene. On March 19, St. Joseph's Day, many families build altars in their homes, and a number of public altars are open at churches and the Piazza d'Italia. Traditionally, food is fed to the poor or any who come to observe the Catholic feast day. Those who visit an altar often receive gifts of fava beans and bread.

Because the observance of St. Joseph's Day comes in the middle of Lent, most of the dishes served are meatless. One of the best known is pasta Milanese, made with a tomato-based sauce often infused with anchovies. Whole fish are frequently baked, and breads are made to look like fish and even alligators. Because the altars are on display for several days, fresh food is often made daily for serving, leaving the ornate breads for decoration only.

2 tbsp. olive oil
1 medium onion, chopped
1 stalk celery, chopped
4 cloves garlic, whole
2 14.5-oz. cans Italian plum
   tomatoes
½ cup fresh fennel bulb, chopped
1 tsp. whole Italian seasoning
Pinch crushed red pepper
1 tsp. sugar

Salt and pepper to taste
6 anchovy fillets, chopped
¼ cup small black olives, pitted
2 tbsp. drained capers
2 tbsp. chopped flat-leaf Italian
   parsley
1 lb. spaghetti
Breadcrumbs, seasoned, and/or
   Parmesan cheese

Heat olive oil in medium, heavy pot. Sauté onion, celery, and whole garlic cloves over medium heat for several minutes until garlic is slightly coloring. Add tomatoes, fennel, Italian seasoning, crushed red pepper, sugar, salt, and pepper. Simmer for about 10 minutes. Add the anchovies, olives, and capers and simmer a few minutes more. Stir in parsley, taste, and adjust seasonings.

Cook spaghetti in large pot of salted, boiling water until al dente. Drain and place in a large pasta bowl, toss with sauce and top with breadcrumbs and/or grated cheese.

Stuffed Whole Cabbage

Ionce came home from a St. Patrick's Day parade weighted down in vegetables, a phenomenon that, as far as I know, is exclusive to New Orleans. Hurled from the floats into my waving arms were cabbages, bell peppers, carrots, potatoes, and even an onion or two. Instead of tossing the stuff, some of it grabbed up from gritty blacktop, I decided to clean it all and cook it. The results were several delicious dinners.

New Orleanians love to stuff things. So do I. Some recipes try my patience, though, such as stuffing individual leaves of cabbage. Therefore, I devised a simple way to do it by using an old technique of stuffing the whole cabbage.

2 cabbages
2 tsp. vegetable or olive oil
I small onion, chopped
½ bell pepper, chopped
I rib celery, chopped
2 cloves garlic, minced
½ lb. ground lean beef
½ lb. ground lean pork
I 14.5-oz. can diced tomatoes seasoned with basil, garlic, and oregano, divided

½ tsp. salt
½ tsp. pepper
I tsp. Creole seasoning
½ cup cooked rice
I egg
½ cup breadcrumbs
4 strips bacon
¼ cup water

Remove any damaged outside leaves of cabbages and slice 1 inch off the top where leaves fold over, leaving the core ends intact. Rinse cabbages and trim the bottom stem end so that the cabbages sit upright. Using a sharp knife or notched utensil such as a grapefruit spoon, dig out the inside of the cabbages, enough to make room for at least 1½ cups of stuffing. Save the scooped-out cabbage for another use such as cole slaw. The outer edge of the cabbages should be about 1 inch thick.

In a large skillet, heat the oil and sauté the onion, bell pepper, celery, and garlic. Add the meat and cook, stirring occasionally, until brown. Add ⅓ of the can of tomatoes, salt, pepper, and Creole seasoning and cook for about

10 minutes. Remove from heat and add rice, egg, and breadcrumbs; mix and stuff into cabbages.

Place cabbages into a large, preferably oval, pot with a rack for steaming. Place 2 strips of bacon over each cabbage. Put remainder of tomatoes and water into bottom of pot. Cover pot and steam cabbages over medium-low heat for 1 hour. Let cabbages set for 10 minutes before serving.

To serve, remove and discard bacon, and cut cabbages lengthwise into quarters. Place a quarter on each plate, and spoon tomato sauce from bottom of pot over it.

Serves 6 to 8.

Stuffed Peppers

When peppers are cheap in the summer, it's fun to buy up a bunch, stuff them, and put them in the freezer. On a rushed weeknight, they're a welcome treat to warm up in the oven. A lot of recipes call for rice, which makes a good filler, but I prefer to get my starch from an accompanying baked macaroni, which goes so well with stuffed peppers. I also like to "Italianize" my peppers by adding some Italian sausage and seasoning. Ciao!

8 medium bell peppers, divided
1 tbsp. vegetable oil
1 onion, chopped
4 green onions, chopped
3 cloves garlic, minced
1 lb. lean ground beef
½ lb. Italian sausage, removed from casings
1 14.5-oz. can Roma tomatoes, diced, or 1 cup chopped fresh ripe tomato
1 tsp. Italian seasoning
Salt, freshly ground pepper, and Creole seasoning to taste
Dash or 2 of Tabasco
1 cup Italian breadcrumbs, divided
⅓ cup Parmesan cheese, grated
3 tbsp. minced Italian flat-leaf parsley
2 eggs, beaten
3 tbsp. butter, cut into small pieces

Slice peppers in halves, cleaning out the white pulp inside. Bring water to a boil in a medium saucepan and parboil 14 of the pepper halves for about 3 minutes. Place on a large baking sheet or pan. Set aside.

Chop the remaining 2 pepper halves. In a large skillet, heat oil and sauté onions, chopped pepper, and garlic. Add ground beef and sausage and sauté until brown and crumbled. Add tomatoes and seasonings. Bring to a simmer, cover, and cook for about 30 minutes, stirring occasionally.

Remove from heat and stir in ½ cup of breadcrumbs, Parmesan cheese, and parsley.

Stir in eggs and mix well. Spoon mixture into pepper shells and top with remaining ½ cup of breadcrumbs and dots of butter. Bake in a preheated 350-degree oven for 30 minutes. These are ready to go, but since I like mine browned on top, I stick them under the broiler for a minute or two.

Serves 6 to 8.

Note: These freeze well.

Red Beans and Rice

After Hurricane Katrina when thousands were dislocated all over the country, many were interviewed about missing New Orleans and how their new lives were going. When asked what they missed most, one of the most recurring answers was the brands of red beans sold in New Orleans and not found in many other places. Yes, the lowly bean ranked right up there with New Orleans' French bread, coffee, crawfish, shrimp, and crabs.

The red bean is king in New Orleans although white beans and dried lima beans run a close second and third. Add rice and you have a complete protein equivalent to meat nutritionally. What is better than something cheap, nutritious, and delicious? Best of all, it's easy to cook when you have something else to do like the wash. Monday was traditional washday in New Orleans, and there was no easier dish to simmer gently on the stove with little attention than a pot of well-seasoned red beans. Meanwhile, the clothes were washed, dried, and put away, a major undertaking before electric washers and dryers.

Seasoning the beans is the key to the dish, and pork adds the most important flavor. Ham, ham bones, and smoked sausage are typical although a variety of smoked pork has been used over the years. If fat is a concern, lean ham and andouille sausage are the best bets, yielding great flavor without high fat. The trinity (onion, bell pepper, and celery) plus garlic do the rest. Make them as spicy as you want and serve over Louisiana rice.

1 lb. dried red beans
3 tbsp. vegetable oil
1 large onion, chopped
1 bell pepper, chopped
2 stalks celery, chopped
1 bunch green onions, chopped
   with green and white divided
3 cloves garlic, crushed
Ham bone, or 8 oz. ham seasoning
   chunks

1 5-inch stick andouille sausage,
   cut into ¼-inch rounds
3 bay leaves
Salt, freshly ground black pepper,
   and Creole seasoning to taste
1 tsp. Italian seasoning
2 tbsp. chopped parsley

Rinse beans and place in a medium bowl. Cover beans well with water and soak overnight or for 6 hours.

Heat oil in a large, heavy pot and sauté onion, bell pepper, celery, and the white part of green onions until soft. Add garlic and sauté a couple of minutes more. Add remaining ingredients except parsley and bring to a boil. Reduce heat to a slow simmer, cover, and cook for two hours, stirring occasionally. If you like more liquid, add it towards the end of cooking. Add green onion tops a few minutes before beans are done and parsley after cooking is complete. Remove bay leaves and serve over white, fluffy rice.

Serves 6.

Liver and Onions

My younger daughter Elizabeth had such an aversion to liver that she once asked, "When you die, what if God serves liver?" I assured her that she would not be made to eat it either on earth or in heaven. But my husband and I gave up one of our favorite dishes, liver and onions, until both girls were away in college. By that time, we were cholesterol conscious and only ate liver on rare occasions. We still indulge occasionally, and I notice more restaurants are putting liver back on menus. It was a favorite in New Orleans for many years and considered to be a great source of iron. Calves' liver is the top choice since it is much tenderer than beef liver. And there's an art to cooking it. It must be cooked done but not a minute more.

I cup flour
I tsp. salt
I tsp. pepper
I ¼ cup vegetable oil

I lb. calves' liver, sliced
2 medium-large onions, sliced ¼ inch thin

On a plate, mix flour, salt, and pepper.

Heat oil in heavy skillet, such as a black, iron skillet.

Dredge liver in flour mixture and brown over medium-high heat until brown on both sides but not cooked through. Remove from skillet. You may have to do this in two batches, or use two skillets. Sauté onions, breaking into rings, until wilted. Return liver to skillet and cover with onions and cook until liver is just done, about 5 minutes on each side. The key to cooking liver is not to overcook. Cook only until blood is coagulated. Serve with grits.

Serves 2 to 3.

Roast Duck

Domestic duck is readily available frozen at grocery stores. The six-pound duck will serve two to four people. This is a French version of whole roasted duck.

1 domestic duck, fresh or frozen, about 6 lb.	2 bay leaves
Salt and pepper	1 small carrot, scraped and sliced
1 large onion, sliced	Thyme leaves
3 cloves garlic, sliced	½ cup white wine
2 stalks celery, sliced	½ cup chicken or duck stock

Thaw duck if necessary. Remove excess fat, rinse well, and pat dry. Prick duck skin all over with a fork, trying not to pierce meat. Season all over with salt and pepper. Place half the onion, garlic, celery, bay leaf, and carrot in cavity of duck. Sprinkle with thyme leaves. Place duck breast side down on a rack in a large baking pan and scatter the remaining vegetables and bay leaf all around the pan. Bake in a preheated 350-degree oven for about 1 hour. Turn duck breast side up. If more than ½ cup of grease has collected, pour some off. Baste with drippings and bake for another hour, or until juices run clear and legs are easy to move. If duck is not browned enough, raise temperature to 400 in the last 20 to 30 minutes of cooking. This will help to make the skin crispy. Transfer duck to a platter, remove vegetables from cavity, and keep duck warm but do not cover or the skin might steam and lose crispiness.

Pour as much grease as possible out of the pan and place pan on a burner on the stove. Over medium-high heat, add the wine and stock. Deglaze the pan, scraping bits from the bottom, and reduce liquid slightly to make a sauce. In a cup, mix 1 heaping tbsp. flour with some of the liquid and stir until smooth. Add to sauce and cook until thickened. Taste and add salt and pepper, if needed. Strain sauce into a serving bowl. To serve, cut duck into serving pieces and serve with sauce.

Note: If you buy a frozen duck, a package of orange sauce may come with it. This can be offered as an alternative to the brown sauce. Just heat and serve in a bowl. If you want to cook the giblets of the duck, simmer with a little onion and celery in water until tender and cut them up to add to wild rice or gravy. Use sparingly because using too much of this can deliver a stronger flavor than you may want.

Roasted Wild Ducks

Ah, for a friend who hunts wild ducks! And even better, one who hunts them but doesn't eat them. I'll take them any time. There's nothing like a generous hunter who shares his limit, especially when it is mallards or teal.

Duck season comes around Thanksgiving and is open at different times during the winter. Sometimes it steals hunters away from the holiday tables, and other times, it's their kill that graces the table. The hunters are cooks, too, and each has his own recipe. Competition runs high on how to prepare the ducks, with secret ingredients ranging from turnips to fruit, and the style of cooking, from iron pots on top of the stove to roasting in the oven.

The most common ways to prepare wild ducks, including teals, mallards, and wood ducks, are in gumbos and roasted slowly in black iron pots. Gumbos generally are dark and rich, made similar to a chicken gumbo. Because wild ducks are leaner and tougher than domestic, longer cooking is required. To pot roast, ducks are cleaned, seasoned well, browned in oil or bacon fat, and simmered for two hours and sometimes more in a small amount of water or wine. Wines of choice are red, such as burgundy, or sherry. Some cooks cover the ducks with slices of bacon and most stuff them with onions, celery, and/or fruit. Turnips are sometimes used to either disguise or enhance the taste, and mushrooms are a favorite addition. Because mallards are larger ducks, they usually are cut into pieces and can be mixed with other smaller ducks when feeding a crowd.

6 to 8 small whole ducks such as teal, or 2 to 3 large ducks such as mallards, cut into pieces (these can be mixed)

Salt, pepper, and cayenne pepper

2 large onions, one cut into chunks and the other sliced, divided

3 stalks celery, sliced, divided

4 cloves garlic, cut in half, divided

½ cup bacon grease or vegetable oil

1 bell pepper, sliced

1 large apple, peeled, cored, and sliced

1 large orange, peeled, cored, and sliced

1 cup red wine such as burgundy or merlot

1 cup mushrooms, white, oyster, shiitake, or portobello, sliced

½ cup green onion tops, sliced

Flat-leaf parsley for garnish, minced

Rinse ducks well, making sure they are free of pinfeathers. Sprinkle well with seasonings and place onion chunks, 1 stalk of sliced celery, and 2 garlic pods in cavities. In a large, heavy Dutch oven or black iron pot, heat the grease or oil and brown ducks on all sides until they are well browned. Place ducks breast side down and cover with sliced onion, bell pepper, remaining celery and garlic, apples, and oranges. Add the wine. Cover pot and place in a 350-degree oven and cook until they are very tender, about 1½ to 2 hours. If more liquid is required and juices are drying up, add more wine, water, or chicken stock. Toward the end of cooking, turn the ducks over to breast side up and add the mushrooms and green onion tops. Cook, uncovered, about 20 more minutes, basting occasionally. The liquid in the pot can be used as is, or more gravy can be made by thickening it with a paste of flour and water and adding water to the desired consistency. When serving, sprinkle with minced parsley. Serve with rice and baked sweet potatoes on the side.

Serves 6.

Deep-fried Turkey

It's a long story, but I'll cut it short. When I was food editor of *The Times-Picayune,* I learned of a man who deep-fried turkeys. I knew I was out of my mind, but I called him anyway. Next thing you know he's deep frying a giant bird in the patio of a French Quarter hotel for me and my husband. I ran the story, despite a few chuckles around the newsroom, just in time for Thanksgiving. On the holiday, we were relaxing in front of the 10:00 P.M. news when a man was interviewed in front of his blazing house. He said, "I'll never use another one of those recipes." (At least he didn't name me or the newspaper.) The next week a letter came from a woman in a nearby town. "Yes, we, too, burned down our house," she said. With that, I became known as the first food editor to burn two houses. Truth be known, only part of the houses burned, and the reason was that the cooks spilled boiling oil into the fire of open burners under carports or overhangs of their houses. The most important part of this recipe is to fry the bird away from any structure and to be careful not to spill the oil into the fire. Later, I had Jim Chehardy, the restaurateur who showed me how, demonstrate to a national group of food writers meeting in New Orleans. Few used the bizarre recipe because in the late '80s, we were ahead of our time. It brings me great pleasure to say that people are now deep-frying turkeys all over the country. And it all began with those creative cooks from Cajun country, who were the first to do it.

1 12-lb. turkey (or between 10 and 15 pounds)
1 turkey injector with poultry marinade (available at grocery stores)
Creole or Cajun seasoning mix, such as Tony Chachere's, or a mixture of cayenne pepper, paprika, white pepper, black pepper, garlic powder, and celery salt
2 to 3 gallons peanut oil

The night before, rinse and pat dry a fresh or thawed turkey. If using a 30-qt. pot, the turkey should be no larger than 15 lb. Using the injector, shoot the marinade through the skin and into the meat all over the turkey, according to package directions. One jar will probably be enough for 2 turkeys. If only using half, pour the half you are using into a bowl and store the rest in the refrigerator. Sprinkle turkey heavily with seasoning inside and out. Wrap in foil, place in a large pan and refrigerate overnight.

About 2 hours before your scheduled mealtime (or $2\frac{1}{2}$ hours if frying 2 turkeys), fill the pot about $\frac{2}{3}$ full of oil. Begin heating the oil over a medium to high flame and heat to 375 degrees, using the thermometer that hooks onto the pot. The amount of oil depends on the size of your turkey. Some people put the turkey in the pot, cover it with water, and measure the water to determine the amount of oil needed. Your cooking oil needs only to cover the turkey. Using too much oil increases the chances of it boiling over onto the flame.

Meanwhile, place turkey on the rack through the breast side so that the breast will go into the pot first. When the oil reaches 375 degrees, place turkey in basket and lower it into the pot. Adjust the fire high enough to return the temperature to 350 degrees as soon as possible. The temperature should be between 350 and 370 degrees during the entire time of cooking. Cooking time is $3\frac{1}{2}$ minutes per pound, or 42 minutes for a 12-pound turkey. Remove the turkey from oil with the grab hook and basket, drain, place on a platter, and let it rest for 15 minutes before serving.

One 12-lb. turkey serves about 6 people.

WARNINGS: Place cooking rig away from any structures, including a car port or overhang of a house. Most fires that have been caused by deep-frying turkeys result from spilling the oil onto the flame. Situate the pot on the burner before adding the oil. Use only enough oil to cover the turkey. Then, keep children and pets away from the pot during the cooking and until the oil has cooled completely. It is a good idea to remove the hot pot from the burner when finished so that nothing will tilt it over. Finally, cover the pot and place it in a safe area.

CHAPTER SIX

Sauces

Fresh Tomato-herb Sauce for Pasta

One of the most delicious parts of visiting Italy is dining on the fresh and simple sauces that Italian cooks love to make. By simply chopping up a few fresh vegetables and using a good-quality olive oil, they can create a masterpiece in minutes. Creole tomato season—May and June—is the time to make this sauce. In Italy, grated cheese is not the norm for serving pasta with garlic and olive oil, or on the fresh tomato sauce. It is certainly a Louisiana tradition and is entirely up to the diner.

6 large red-ripe tomatoes, preferably Creole or plum (about 3 lb.)

½ cup extra-virgin olive oil

3 green onions, chopped

1 stalk celery, chopped

3 cloves garlic, minced

½ tsp. sugar

2 tbsp. fresh basil leaves, chopped

2 tbsp. fresh oregano leaves, chopped

2 tbsp. Italian parsley leaves, chopped

Salt and freshly ground pepper to taste

1 lb. pasta of choice, fresh preferred

Grated cheese, preferably Parmigiano Reggiano, optional

Drop tomatoes into boiling water for about 3 seconds one at a time and pull the peeling off with a knife. It should just slide off. Slice tomatoes in half horizontally and squeeze to remove seeds. Chop and set aside.

Heat olive oil and sauté onions and celery until soft. Add garlic and sauté a minute more. Add fresh tomatoes and sugar and cook over medium heat for about 5 minutes. Add herbs and seasonings and cook a few minutes longer. Adjust seasonings and serve over cooked, drained pasta. Add cheese to your liking.

Serves 4.

Hollandaise Sauce

What is more luscious than a hollandaise sauce over eggs, vegetables, and fish? What scares most cooks is the threat of curdling, a strong possibility if you overheat the ingredients. The key is keeping your heat very low and stirring the ingredients in a double boiler. Practice makes perfect, and eventually you will get the hang of it.

4 egg yolks
1 lb. butter (4 sticks)

5 tsp. lemon juice

Beat yolks for 1 minute in the top of a double boiler over low heat. Add $1/2$ stick (4 tbsp.) butter and melt slowly, beating. In a glass measuring cup, gently melt the remaining $3^1/2$ sticks of butter in the microwave, being careful not to boil or separate, stirring frequently. Add slowly to the egg mixture, stirring constantly, in the double boiler over low heat. Add lemon juice, 1 tsp. at a time, while adding melted butter. Continue to warm and stir the sauce until all is combined and thickened. To keep the temperature low, move the pot on and off the fire. This is best served immediately. If you must hold the sauce before serving, remove from the heat and reheat over very low heat, stirring.
Makes about 2 cups.

Horseradish Sauce

This is a quick way to make a horseradish sauce without starting from scratch grating the horseradish. Make sure you buy the fresh refrigerated kind of horseradish, which is much fresher than the jarred ones with preservatives. This is good served with boiled beef, oysters, and shrimp.

3 tbsp. fresh horseradish (in refrigerated jars)
4 tbsp. ketchup

3 tbsp. Creole mustard
1 tsp. lemon juice

Mix all together and keep refrigerated.

CHAPTER SEVEN

Breakfast

Buttermilk Biscuits

Too much handling is the fatal blow to biscuit making. You should never knead biscuit dough because it makes the biscuits tough. Yet, a smooth consistency is important, too. For years, I used too much flour, and the dough was too dry to mix well. Enough moisture is the key to forming a soft and pliable ball of dough ready to roll out. I also prefer buttermilk to plain milk because the biscuits have a better flavor. A bit of sugar and the right amount of salt are crucial as well.

2 cups all-purpose flour	**½ tsp. sugar**
2½ tsp. baking powder	**⅓ cup shortening**
¼ tsp. baking soda	**I cup buttermilk**
½ tsp. salt	

Sift dry ingredients into a large bowl. Cut in shortening with a pastry cutter until only pea-size lumps remain. Gradually stir in buttermilk and combine until all ingredients are wet. With well-floured hands, roll dough into a ball. Do not knead, but try to get a smooth consistency. The less you handle, the better the biscuits. Generously flour a board and rolling pin. Roll out dough to ½ inch thick. Flour a biscuit cutter and cut biscuits. Place them side to side on a lightly greased pan. Preheat oven to 400 degrees and bake biscuits for 15 to 20 minutes or until browning slightly on top and bottom. Do not overbake.

Makes about 16 biscuits if using a 2-inch cutter.

Pain Perdu
(LOST BREAD)

I know that people love French toast all over the country, but here we call it pain perdu, or lost bread. And our version in south Louisiana is more luscious. We tend to use thick slices of leftover French bread, well soaked not in just egg and milk, but sugar and vanilla and sometimes even a shot of brandy. Instead of regular pancake syrup, we might use pure cane syrup. Children love this for breakfast, and it's all part of the early start we give them in developing taste buds and learning to relish good food.

I'm not sure why, but French bread is different here. Some say it's the water that goes into it. I'm inclined to think it is the artisan recipes and baking techniques brought here by the German bakers whose families still influence our daily bread. The real thing has no preservatives, the reason that it goes stale overnight, which is why Creoles bought fresh bread first thing every morning. Whatever was left went into the pain perdu and bread pudding the next day. Heaven forbid that anything was wasted!

Pain perdu is French for the age-old technique of reviving stale bread. The recipe appears all over Europe under different names. In England, it is known as the poor knights of Windsor and is called the same thing in native languages of Holland, Sweden, Denmark, and Germany. Some histories trace it to ancient Roman days where it was considered a dessert.

Like bread pudding, pain perdu is a simple dish in which stale bread is soaked in an egg-milk mixture and sautéed in butter until golden brown. It is served with a sprinkling of confectioners' sugar and drizzled with syrup. Also, like bread pudding, it can be dressed up for the finest occasion with little effort. Fresh berries make a quick sauce for a colorful topping, and some cooks sandwich a fruit filling between slices of bread before soaking and sautéing them.

8 slices dry French bread, 1 inch
   thick, 1 to 2 days old
3 eggs
1½ cups milk
3 tbsp. sugar

1½ tsp. vanilla
Pinch nutmeg
3 tbsp. butter
Confectioners' sugar
Louisiana cane syrup

Slice bread into rounds. In a large bowl, beat eggs, add milk and sugar, and mix thoroughly. Stir in vanilla and nutmeg. Place bread in mixture and soak for about 2 minutes. In a large skillet, heat half the butter to medium-hot. Drain 4 slices of bread and sauté about 2 minutes on each side until golden brown. Repeat with remaining butter and bread slices. Drain on paper towels and sprinkle with confectioners' sugar. A small strainer works best for sifting and sprinkling the sugar. Serve with cane syrup on the table.

Serves 4.

The following recipe makes a dressed-up but easy version to serve at brunches.

Pain Perdu with Berry Sauce

I recipe for pain perdu (above)
3 cups berries such as strawberries
   or blueberries
I cup sugar
I cup water

2 tbsp. Grand Marnier or other
   orange-flavored liqueur
I tbsp. cornstarch
2 cups whipped cream, optional

Prepare pain perdu according to directions above. Keep warm until serving.

To prepare the sauce, place rinsed and dried berries in a medium saucepan with sugar, water, and liqueur and stir to mix. Add cornstarch and mix. Heat gently, stirring occasionally, until sauce has thickened. Cool to room temperature. This can be made ahead, refrigerated, and brought to room temperature. Serve in a bowl as an optional topping. In another bowl, place freshly whipped cream flavored with a little sugar and vanilla. You can place cane syrup and sifted confectioners' sugar in other bowls, letting guests choose their toppings.

Note: If strawberries are large, cut in half or slice. If using blueberries that are not very sweet, you may have to add extra sugar.

Fig Preserves

Many a breakfast in the South features fig preserves on hot biscuits. Beside a slab of country ham, there may be no better eating on the planet. We Southerners tend to grow our own figs in the backyard. And when they ripen, there are more than anyone knows what to do with. Making fig preserves is relatively easy. It's just the canning part that takes a while. Some people skip the water bath and simply pour the hot preserves into sterilized jars. This is safe enough if you plan to eat them in a reasonable amount of time. If, however, you want to make and keep enough for a year or two, you probably want to take the precaution of boiling the finished jars in a water bath. Use a jar to make fig cake (see index for recipe).

4 lb. figs	**2 cups water**
4 cups sugar	**I lemon, sliced thin**

Rinse figs gently and set aside. To make a syrup with sugar and water, place both in a large saucepan and bring to a boil. Cook until mixture becomes clear and begins to thicken, about 15 minutes. Add lemon slices and figs and simmer until tender, about 30 minutes. Pour into sterilized jars, leaving $1/2$-inch space at the top, and process in a hot water bath for 20 minutes.

Makes about 6 half pints.

Pumpkin Bread

A handy use of pumpkin is baking it into small loaves of nutty pumpkin bread, just right for take-alongs to holiday parties or little gifts to friends. Make multiple batches and stack them in the freezer, too. Pumpkin, like bananas, makes nut bread extra moist.

3 cups sugar
4 eggs
2 cups pumpkin, puréed
3⅓ cups flour
2 tsp. baking soda

1½ tsp. salt
1 tsp. nutmeg
1 tsp. cinnamon
⅔ cup water
1 cup pecans, chopped

Mix sugar and eggs in electric mixer. Blend in pumpkin. In a separate bowl, sift together all dry ingredients and add gradually to the pumpkin mixture. Add water and blend until mixture is smooth. Stir in pecans.

Bake in a preheated 350-degree oven in two slightly greased 9-by-5-by-3-inch loaf pans for about 1 hour or until a toothpick comes out of the center clean. Cool briefly in pans, then transfer to wire racks to cook completely.

Makes 2 loaves.

Note: Recipe will make a half-dozen mini-loaves.

Eggs Sardou

One of this city's grandest pleasures is dining midday on glorious egg dishes. None is more popular than our own eggs Sardou. Antoine Alciatore, founder of Antoine's Restaurant, created the dish for a dinner he hosted for the French playwright Victorien Sardou.

In New Orleans, eggs are coupled with veal and pork, spinach and artichokes. If you must tamper with the near perfect eggs Benedict, my preferences are artichokes or spinach, both of which pair exceptionally well with runny eggs. Technically, Antoine's Sardou does not place spinach on the artichoke bottoms but instead uses anchovy fillets and sliced truffle. Perhaps because of local tastes and the accessibility of less costly ingredients, spinach is the common substitute, which I will take any time.

4 tbsp. butter, divided	8 artichoke bottoms, freshly
I small onion, chopped	cooked or canned
2 9-oz. bags fresh, washed spinach	2 tbsp. white vinegar
2 tbsp. flour	8 eggs
I cup heavy cream	2 cups hollandaise sauce (see
Salt and pepper	index for recipe)
Pinch nutmeg	

In a large pot, melt 2 tbsp. of the butter and sauté onion. Add spinach, half at a time, and cover to wilt over a low fire, stirring frequently. Sauté spinach until wilted and just done. This takes just a few minutes. Set aside.

In a small pot, melt remaining 2 tbsp. of butter and turn off heat. Stir or whisk in the flour until mixed thoroughly and add gradually the heavy cream, mixing until smooth. Return to heat and, stirring constantly over low heat, cook until thickened. Do not boil. Add salt and pepper to taste and nutmeg. Stir into the spinach and set aside.

Prepare artichoke bottoms and keep warm.

Heat 2 quarts of water with salt and vinegar in a large frying pan. When it reaches a gentle simmer, place eggs, one at a time, in a cup and slide carefully into water. Cook for about 3 to 4 minutes until the white is done and yolk is still runny. It is easier to cook 4 at a time and hold them in a warm place while cooking the other 4.

To assemble, place a fourth of the creamed spinach on each plate and top with 2 artichoke bottoms. Place a poached egg in each artichoke bottom, and top all with hollandaise sauce.

Serves 4.

Eggs Benedict

I love the simplicity of eggs Benedict. Toasted English muffins topped with ham or Canadian bacon, poached eggs, and hollandaise sauce is all required, and it's a dish fit for a king. Legend has it that the creation originated at New York's Delmonico's Restaurant when regular customers Mr. and Mrs. LeGrand Benedict complained there was nothing new on the lunch menu. The restaurant's maitre d' and Mrs. Benedict began discussing possibilities, and eggs Benedict was born.

4 English muffins   **8 eggs**
8 slices ham or Canadian bacon   **2 cups hollandaise sauce (see**
2 tbsp. white vinegar   **index for recipe)**
Salt

Divide English muffins into halves and place on a cookie sheet. Place ham or Canadian bacon in a skillet. Set aside.

In a wide pan such as a large frying pan, bring 2 quarts of water, the vinegar, and salt to a gentle simmer. One at a time, place an egg in a small coffee cup, hold it close to the water and let it slide in. Do not crowd the pan. You may be more comfortable doing 4 at a time. Simmer until the white forms a thin veil over the yolks, about 3 to 4 minutes. When done, with the yolk still runny, lift them out one at a time with a slotted spoon or skimmer. Pat dry with a paper towel and keep warm.

Heat a broiler and toast English muffins until lightly browned. At the same time, heat ham or Canadian bacon.

To assemble, place 2 muffin halves on each plate, top each with a ham slice and then a poached egg. Drizzle hollandaise over all. Serve immediately with a pepper mill and Tabasco at the table.

Serves 4.

CHAPTER EIGHT

Desserts

Fig Cake

An extra jar of fig preserves begs to become fig cake. Moist and aromatic, this cake originates with summer fig season when trees all over New Orleans are laden with the brownish-pink fruit. Pick all you can before the birds get to them, and what you don't eat, turn into preserves. The cake screams for a glass of milk. It's also meant for lunch boxes.

2 cups all-purpose flour, sifted
½ tsp. salt
1 tsp. baking soda
1 tsp. cinnamon
½ tsp. allspice
½ tsp. nutmeg
1 ¼ cups sugar

1 stick butter, softened
2 eggs
1 tsp. vanilla extract
1 cup buttermilk
1 cup fig preserves
1 cup chopped pecans
Whipped cream, optional

Preheat oven to 350 degrees. Lightly grease and flour a tube, Bundt, or large loaf pan.

Mix flour, salt, baking soda, cinnamon, allspice, and nutmeg and set aside.

In a mixer, cream the sugar and butter. Add eggs, one at a time, and beat well. Add vanilla and mix well. Alternately, add dry ingredients and buttermilk and beat on high speed for 3 minutes. Fold in fig preserves and pecans. Pour into pan and bake for 45 minutes to 1 hour or until a toothpick stuck in the middle comes out clean. Cool for 10 minutes in pan. Remove from pan and cool completely on wire rack. This is good served with freshly whipped cream on top.

Serves 10 to 12.

Strawberry Shortcake

There's nothing like a Louisiana strawberry, and my favorite way to eat them is as an old-fashioned strawberry shortcake. Although some local farmers have planted West Coast varieties to compete with the large California berries, everybody knows the Louisiana berry is redder, sweeter, and juicier than most. Part of that is because they are not picked early and shipped. The freshest seem to be at the roadside stands, especially around Hammond and Ponchatoula where they are grown, or at a farmers' market. A few grocery stores stock the native berries, too. Did you know that strawberries got their name from the pine straw collected from the woods to place around the strawberry plants?

1 cup flour	5 tbsp. cold milk
¼ tsp. salt	2 pints Louisiana strawberries
1 tsp. baking powder	Whipped cream or topping
3 tbsp. shortening	

In a medium bowl, sift dry ingredients and mix together. Cut in shortening. Gradually add milk, mixing with a fork until dough comes together. Roll into ball and place in refrigerator for 30 minutes. Roll out and cut into circles like biscuits about ¼ inch thick. Place on greased cookie sheet and bake at 425 degrees until lightly browned, 10 to 12 minutes. You will have 8 to 10 shortcakes.

Rinse berries gently and dry on paper towels.

To serve, make 2 layers of shortcakes topped with berries and top all with whipped cream or topping.

Serves 4.

Strawberry-topped Cheesecake

Louisiana strawberry season thrills me to the bone. It's at a beautiful time of year when flowers are budding and everything is green. Nothing tastes as fresh as OUR strawberries. They come straight from the farm with no travel time or cold storage to ruin them. All kinds of berries go with cheesecake, none better than strawberries. This is a New York-style cheesecake that is delicious by itself but even better when Creolized by our very own berries.

GRAHAM CRUST:
1½ cups graham cracker crumbs
6 tbsp. butter, melted
⅓ cup sugar
Cinnamon

FILLING:
2 8-oz. packages cream cheese
2 eggs
⅔ cup sugar
1 tsp. vanilla
Juice from ½ large lemon

SOUR CREAM TOPPING:
2 cups sour cream
5 tbsp. sugar
1 tsp. vanilla extract
1 tsp. almond extract

STRAWBERRY SAUCE:
1 pint strawberries, mashed
    slightly with a fork
⅓ cup sugar
1 tbsp. cornstarch
½ cup water
2 tbsp. Grand Marnier or other
    orange-flavored liqueur,
    optional

To make crust: Combine all ingredients and press into an 8- or 9-inch pie plate.

To make filling: Let cream cheese come to room temperature. In a mixer, beat eggs. Add sugar and mix well. Add cream cheese and beat until smooth, about 5 minutes. Add vanilla and lemon juice and mix well. Pour into crust. Bake for 20 minutes at 375 degrees. Let stand for 15 minutes.

Increase oven temperature to 425 degrees. Mix sour cream topping ingredients, spread on top of the cheesecake and bake another 10 minutes.

Let cheesecake cool before adding strawberry sauce. Sauce can be poured over the entire cake or added to individual slices when served.

To prepare the strawberry sauce, rinse and pat berries dry. Remove stems. Mash slightly with a fork to release some of the juice. Place in a medium saucepan and mix with sugar. In a small bowl, mix cornstarch with water and add to strawberries. Stir in Grand Marnier if using. Heat gently, stirring occasionally, until sauce bubbles slightly and has thickened. Cool to room temperature. This can be made ahead, refrigerated, and brought to room temperature.

Serves 8 to 10.

Fresh Blueberry Pie

One of the newest and most delicious crops to adorn Louisiana in recent years is blueberries, now a constant on the North Shore and other parts of the state and south Mississippi. June is the big month though they start in May and can linger into July. The good part is that they can be frozen easily and used throughout the year. To my mind, there is nothing more enticing than a warm berry pie a la mode. The piping dark berries and cold vanilla ice cream are a match made in heaven. I buy them by the crate during the season and freeze them in pint-size freezer bags. You should not wash them until you are ready to use them. Thaw and rinse four cups and a fresh blueberry pie can be on your table in the middle of January. Another trick of mine is using ready-made refrigerated pie crusts. Make them from scratch if you wish but a pie is only minutes away when you use these handy time savers.

2 pie crusts, refrigerated ready
  made or homemade
1 cup sugar
¼ cup flour
¼ tsp. salt
½ tsp. cinnamon
5 cups fresh blueberries (or

thawed from frozen), rinsed
  and drained
1 tsp. grated lemon rind
1 tbsp. lemon juice
3 tbsp. butter, cut into dots
1 egg white

Preheat oven to 400 degrees. Place 1 crust into a 9- or 10-inch pie plate and set aside.

In a medium bowl, combine sugar, flour, salt, and cinnamon. Add blueberries and lemon rind and toss gently to mix well. Spoon into crust and spread evenly. Drizzle lemon juice over berries and dot with butter. Place top crust on and pinch edge of crusts together, creating an attractive rim. Beat egg white and brush pie with enough to moisten. Cut several slits in top crust to allow steam to escape.

Place a sheet of tin foil below the rack the pie will bake on just in case any juice should bubble over. Bake pie for about 40 minutes or until it is bubbly and brown on top. Cool for 30 minutes or more and serve warm with vanilla ice cream.

Serves 6 to 8.

Bread Pudding

It's hard to believe that the lowliest dessert on every poor man's table has become a must at most upscale New Orleans restaurants. Bread pudding was created to use up leftover stale bread so as not to waste even a morsel of food. French bread, milk, and eggs are the basics, flavored by vanilla and sprinkled with raisins. But local cooks have a way of elevating simple food to greatness, and the buttery sauce spiked with brandy or whiskey is the crowning glory. New versions infuse bread pudding with many ingredients — white chocolate, milk chocolate, nuts, coconut, and a variety of fruits. A bread pudding soufflé became the most popular dessert at Commander's Palace.

Ironically, this dessert is built on the reputation of New Orleans' famous French bread, said to be unlike any other in the United States. Bakers from France and Germany set the standard in the nineteenth century, and some of the same families still produce the artisan bread that make yet another legendary dish, the po-boy, a local wonder duplicated no where else.

4 eggs
5 cups milk
1½ cups sugar
2 tbsp. vanilla
1 loaf French bread, one day old,
cut or broken into chunks
½ cup raisins
½ cup pecans
2 tbsp. butter, cubed

In a large bowl, beat eggs lightly and whisk in milk, sugar, and vanilla. Add bread and soak for 30 minutes, stirring occasionally. Add raisins and place in a 9-by-13-inch baking dish. Top with pecans and dot with butter. (Pecans stay crisper when on top.) Bake in a preheated 350-degree oven until bubbly and brown on top, about 1 hour. If you like the top well browned, run the dish under the broiler for 5 minutes. Let the pudding set for about 15 to 30 minutes, cut into squares and serve with warm bourbon sauce.
Serves 6 to 8.

Bourbon Sauce

1 stick butter	**2 egg yolks, beaten**
¾ cup sugar	**½ cup bourbon**

Combine butter and sugar in double boiler and heat, stirring, until sugar dissolves. Remove upper pot from fire and add egg yolks gradually, whisking briskly, so that eggs do not curdle. Cool for a few minutes and add bourbon, whisking. Pour over bread pudding when serving.

Old-fashioned Vanilla Custard Ice Cream

How lucky we are to have snowball stands all over town and a zillion flavors to choose from. But another summer treat that is equally tempting is homemade ice cream, once the centerpiece of outdoor summer parties yet now on its way to the "lost recipe" files.

When big families got together, the women were in charge of cooking the custard and chilling it down for the tall silver cylinders that fit into wooden buckets. Sometimes fresh strawberries or peaches were sliced or mashed to add to the mix. Then the men took over, packing the ice and salt around the cylinder and turning the crank by hand. Young males eager to get in on the action could attend the early churning, but as the cream grew thick, it took the stronger muscles of the elders. Removing the cylinder was a tedious task because any salt infiltration would ruin the batch. Then came the delight of scooping the thick, creamy frozen custard off the paddle just as soon as it was pulled from the tub.

The joys of the backyard ice cream party are mostly memories today, but the good news is that the experience of freshly churned ice cream can be duplicated easily using the same recipes in chic new machines. Whip them up in the kitchen or take them to the backyard for a picnic.

2 qt. whole milk
6 eggs, 3 of them separated
1 ½ cups sugar
2 heaping tbsp. flour
1 tbsp. vanilla

1 pint cream (breakfast or half-and-half), or 1 14-oz. can sweetened condensed milk (For a richer, sweeter ice cream, use sweetened condensed milk.)

Pour milk into a large saucepan and place over low heat. While milk is warming, beat 3 eggs and 3 egg yolks well in a medium bowl. Beat the 3 whites until stiff and set aside. Add sugar and flour to whole eggs and yolks and then a little of the warm milk. Add mixture to pot of warm milk. Stir over medium heat to boiling point. When it reaches a boil, boil for 1 minute or until mixture coats the spoon. Remove from fire and beat in stiff egg whites, vanilla, and cream or condensed milk. Cool, whisking occasionally, and refrigerate until ready to freeze. Mixture should be chilled before freezing. Freeze in an ice cream freezer according to manufacturer's directions.

Cup Custard

During my college days at Ole Miss, I visited the home of a New Orleans friend whose parents graciously wined and dined us at Commander's Palace. It was my first time to eat cup custard, also known as caramel custard. It was divine. I loved the creamy custard with the dark syrupy caramel on top, so different from the custards back home. My family made English custards that sometimes had little meringue islands floating on top.

Later, when I learned to make flan, I saw the similarities in the Spanish baked custard and the French crème caramel that found their way to white tablecloths in New Orleans restaurants. The caramelizing of sugar that first hardened and then melted like a sauce over the custard was both French and Spanish like the city that was to become my home.

The best part about cup custard is that it is simple to make and can be made ahead. Ingredients are simple—eggs, milk or cream, and sugar with a vanilla flavoring and a possible pinch of salt and/or nutmeg. Cup custard can be made without the caramelized sugar and served in its baking cups. However, the extra step of caramelizing sugar is well worth the trouble. For an elegant touch, serve fresh, sweetened berries on the side. The contrasting colors of blueberries and raspberries brighten the neutral shades of the custard and add a tanginess to the taste.

3 eggs	2 cups half-and-half
I egg yolk	I tsp. vanilla extract
I cup sugar	I tsp. water
Pinch salt	

Preheat oven to 350 degrees.

Beat eggs and yolk with a whisk or in a mixer until foamy. Add ½ cup sugar and salt and whisk. Gradually add half-and-half and then vanilla and mix well. Set aside.

In a small saucepan, heat remaining ½ cup of sugar with water, stirring constantly, until mixture is caramelized and a medium-brown color. Pour a little into 6 oven-proof ramekins or dessert cups, quickly swirling it across the bottom of each cup.

Divide egg mixture equally into ramekins and set into a large baking pan with 3-inch sides. Place pan in oven and pour warm water from a pitcher into the pan to a 1 inch depth. Bake for 1 hour or until a knife inserted in the center of custard comes out clean. Cool and store in the refrigerator.

When ready to serve, run a knife around each ramekin to loosen the custard and invert on a small plate. Drizzle caramel over the custard.

Serves 6.

Crème Brûlée

Crème brûlée is characterized by its brittle caramelized topping. There are several ways to achieve this crisp lid. You can place ramekins containing the dessert under a broiler until the top becomes caramelized and crisp. Or, you can play like a chef and use a salamander or blowtorch. The literal translation of crème brûlée is "burnt cream." For an elegant touch, serve fresh, sweetened berries on the side.

Yolks of 6 large eggs
½ cup sugar
2½ cups half-and-half

1 tsp. vanilla extract
½ cup brown sugar

Preheat oven to 325 degrees. In a medium bowl, whisk egg yolks until light. Add sugar and whisk well. Gradually add half-and-half, whisking, and add vanilla extract. Pour into 6 oven-proof ramekins or dessert cups. Place ramekins in a large baking pan with 3-inch sides and place in oven. Pour warm water into the pan to a 1 inch depth. Bake for approximately 30 minutes or until the custards are barely set. Cool completely and then refrigerate.

Just before you are ready to serve, sprinkle custards with the brown sugar. Place directly under a preheated broiler and broil on high heat until sugar has caramelized and is brown. Watch this closely or it will burn. Serve immediately, or refrigerate briefly—no longer than 1 hour—before serving. Alternately, a kitchen blowtorch can be used to brown the sugar.

Serves 6.

Strawberry Custard Pie

Strawberries make great pies, especially the small, sweet variety known in Louisiana. If you're only finding large, less juicy and less sweet ones, they will have to be sliced and sweetened. If they are the traditional type, no slicing or sweetening is necessary. This custard pie can be topped with either meringue or whipped cream.

2 9-inch deep-dish pie crust
 shells, homemade, frozen, or
 refrigerated, baked
2 pints Louisiana strawberries,
 rinsed and patted dry (if large,
 slice and toss with 2 tbsp. sugar
 if needed)

I qt. milk
⅔ cup sugar
2 heaping tbsp. flour
I egg plus 5 egg yolks, beaten
2 tsp. vanilla, divided
I cup whipping cream
I tsp. powdered sugar

Bake pie shells and cool. Prepare berries. Set aside.

In a double boiler, heat milk to hot but not boiling. Mix sugar and flour and stir into milk. Add a little milk mixture to eggs and stir in. Add egg mixture very gradually into milk mixture, stirring constantly. Cook custard over medium heat until thick, stirring constantly, about 10 minutes. When thickened, remove from heat and cool. When cool, add 1 tsp. vanilla and strawberries. Fill pie shells with strawberry custard. Whip cream until peaks form. Add 1 tsp. vanilla and powdered sugar and whip briefly. Spread onto pie. Refrigerate.

Serves 8.

Note: If meringue topping is preferred, beat the 5 egg whites until foamy. Add a pinch of cream of tartar and continue beating, gradually adding ¼ cup confectioners' sugar until stiff peaks form. Spread onto pie and place pie in a 350-degree oven until lightly browned on top, about 10 minutes.

Lemon Ice

I have two favorite flavors, lemon and chocolate, and I cannot under any circumstances pick one over the other. I will say that in summer, lemon gets a slight edge. There is something about the sharpness of flavor in a lemon curd or lemon pie that takes it over the top. Add ice and there is no outdoing it on a hot New Orleans day. This recipe gives you that wonderful lemon curd flavor and at the same time cools you down to a happy comfort zone.

4 cups water
2 cups sugar

1 tbsp. grated lemon zest
1 cup lemon juice

Combine water and sugar and bring to a boil. Boil for 5 minutes. Cool. Add lemon peel and juice. Freeze in an ice cream freezer according to manufacturer's directions.

Bananas Foster

Bananas were shipped through the New Orleans port in such quantity back in the '50s (and still are) that famed restaurateur Owen Brennan challenged his chef Paul Blange to create a spectacular banana dessert. And that he did.

The French chef came up with a simple recipe of mostly sugar, spirits, and bananas. The crowning glory came when a match was struck and the rich sauce went up in flames at the diners' tables. As Brennan's is prone to do, it named the creation after a person, Richard Foster, a frequent customer who was an official on the New Orleans crime commission. Today, Brennan's is said to flambé 35,000 pounds of bananas per year while the international reputation has placed the dish on menus far and wide.

The key is starting with ripe bananas just beginning to spot. Cut off the tips because they are bitter. Then follow the directions below, but just remember to flambé the dessert away from the heat by removing the pan from the flame when igniting. Do not flambé near fabrics or any other flammable objects or stand too close to the pan. It is safe to use long fireplace matches when lighting the sauce.

6 bananas	½ cup dark rum, divided
½ cup butter	⅓ cup banana liqueur
1 cup brown sugar	Vanilla ice cream
1 tsp. cinnamon	

Slice bananas lengthwise and in half. In a chafing dish set over Sterno® (canned heat), melt butter. Mix brown sugar and cinnamon and stir into butter until sugar is melted. Add ¼ cup of rum and banana liqueur. Cook for several minutes until brown and syrupy. Add bananas and cook a few minutes more, until the bananas are soft and beginning to brown. Add remaining rum, let rum heat, but do not stir. Remove from fire, tip the pan to the side and, with a long taper match, ignite the sauce. Baste the bananas with the sauce. When the flames subside, spoon the bananas over ice cream in individual bowls. Serve immediately.

Serves 6.

Crêpes Fitzgerald

Flaming desserts are a specialty in some of New Orleans' oldest restaurants. None is better than crêpes Fitzgerald during strawberry season when the fresh berries come from Louisiana. Cream cheese-stuffed crêpes are blanketed in a fresh strawberry sauce spiked with orange or cherry liqueur. A tableside performance is fun to do at home, especially during the holidays. All it takes is a chafing dish and a can of Sterno®, but remember to remove the pan from the flame when igniting. Use long fireplace matches to ignite and make sure no flammable fabrics are nearby.

CRÊPES:
2 large eggs
I cup whole milk
½ cup water
Pinch salt
I tbsp. butter, melted
I cup flour
Vegetable oil for cooking

CREAM CHEESE FILLING:
3 tbsp. sugar

8 oz. cream cheese, at room
    temperature
2 tbsp. orange-flavored liqueur

STRAWBERRY SAUCE:
¼ cup butter
½ cup sugar
3 pints strawberries, cleaned and
    halved
¼ cup strawberry- or orange-
    flavored liqueur

To make the crêpes: Beat the eggs in a bowl. Beat in the milk, water, salt, and butter. Then add the flour gradually until mixture is smooth. This can be done in a blender or by hand. Let mixture stand for about 20 minutes. When ready to cook, stir again and measure 3 tbsp. batter for the first crêpe. Brush a crêpe pan or small non-stick skillet lightly with oil and heat to very hot. You may want to use two pans at once. Cook each crêpe separately, swirling the batter around to make a thin pancake. Cook until bubbles form and the underside is brown. Flip and cook other side, which should brown only slightly and be used as the inside. Each side takes less than a minute. Place cooked crêpes on paper towels. (Crêpes can be made in advance, separated by sheets of wax paper and frozen.) Makes about 2 dozen crêpes.

To make the cream cheese filling: Combine all ingredients. Fill 16 crêpes with 3 tbsp. of the filling by placing filling on one side of crêpe and rolling up. These can be made ahead of time and placed in the refrigerator. (From this recipe, you will have a few leftover crêpes to freeze.)

To make the strawberry sauce: Melt the butter in a chafing dish set over Sterno®. Add sugar and stir until dissolved. Add strawberries and cook for several minutes. Add liqueur and cook a few minutes more. Tip the pan, removing it from the Sterno®, and flambé with a long taper match. Stir until flames go out.

To serve: Place room temperature filled crêpes on plates, 2 per serving. Pour warm strawberry sauce over.

Serves 8.

Grilled Pineapple

Sometimes it's fun to grill your whole dinner, vegetables in a grilling basket alongside your meat. But what about dessert? Here's one that is not only easy and delicious, it's good for you, too.

1 fresh pineapple	**Cinnamon**
½ cup rum	**Nutmeg**
¼ cup brown sugar	**Vanilla ice cream, optional**

Peel and slice pineapple, or buy fresh pineapple already prepared at the grocery store.

Make sure the slices are at least ¼ inch thick. About an hour before you are ready to grill pineapple, mix the rum, brown sugar, cinnamon, and nutmeg together. Place pineapple slices flat in a container, drizzle with rum sauce and turn, coating both sides. Marinate for about 1 hour.

Prepare a medium-hot charcoal fire and spray a clean grill with PAM®. Place pineapple slices about 6 inches over the coals and cook until light brown on each side, about 5 minutes per side. Serve in bowls topped with vanilla ice cream, or cut into chunks and serve over vanilla ice cream.

Serves 6.

Caramel Pie

This was my favorite pie as a child, and I can't say that I like any better to this day. My mother, Doris Blair, made the best pies—and biscuits—of anyone I have ever known. Her crusts melted in your mouth, and the custard fillings were beyond belief. I singled out caramel over chocolate and lemon as my very favorite and thus called for it on all special occasions. It is a pie of simple ingredients, the kind she always had on hand and never had to go to the store in order to make. Sugar, eggs, flour, milk and there you have it, the kind of recipe home cooks generally made before the days of easy accessibility to exotic ingredients. Caramelizing, or the browning of sugar, was a popular way to get the maximum flavor from a dessert. Take pralines, for instance. Or caramel cup custard. Or caramel cakes and pies.

My mother may have gotten this recipe from the Mid-South Fair in Memphis. This massive annual event is spread out over acres of buildings and fields in the middle of the city. Our favorite was the Women's Building in which miniature pies were sold by the thousands. Most were custard-style of good British heritage, and every year I chose caramel. It was a tough decision that I labored over mightily, but in the end, it was the same every time—caramel!

CRUST:
1½ cups flour
½ tsp. salt
½ cup shortening
5 tbsp. ice water

FILLING:
3 egg yolks
2 tbsp. sugar
2 tbsp. flour
2 cups milk

1 cup sugar
1 tsp. vanilla

MERINGUE:
1 tbsp. cornstarch
2 tbsp. cold water
½ cup boiling water
3 egg whites
6 tbsp. sugar
Dash of salt
1 tsp. vanilla

To make crust: Sift flour with salt into a medium bowl. Cut in shortening with a pastry cutter or two knives until the mixture is slightly coarse. Add ice water 1 tbsp. at a time and mix gradually with a fork. When pastry begins to stick together, form a ball with your hands, pressing the dough together. Refrigerate for 30 minutes. Roll out on floured board to ⅛ inch thickness. Place crust in a 9-inch pie pan. Preheat oven to 425 degrees. Pierce pie shell in three places and weight the crust down with another pie plate. Bake for 12 minutes and remove the top plate. Lower temperature to 350 and continue baking until the crust is golden brown. Set aside.

To make filling: Whisk the egg yolks briefly in a bowl, add 2 tbsp. sugar and flour and blend. Heat the milk and gradually pour into the egg mixture, whisking together. Set aside.

In a medium saucepan, heat 1 cup sugar slowly, stirring constantly. Cook until sugar is brown and add egg-milk mixture. Mix well and cook, stirring, until thick. Add vanilla. Pour into pie crust.

To make meringue: Blend cornstarch and cold water in saucepan. Add boiling water and cook, stirring until clear and thickened. Let stand until completely cold. With electric mixer at high speed, beat egg whites until foamy, gradually add sugar, and beat until stiff but not dry. Turn mixer to low speed and add salt and vanilla. Gradually beat in cold cornstarch mixture. Turn mixer again to high speed and beat well. Spread meringue on filled pie and bake in a preheated 350-degree oven for about 10 minutes.

Serves 6 to 8.

Pecan Pie

If there were ever a diet-buster, it's pecan pie. It's one of those things, like fried chicken and fudge, that I eat only once or twice a year. Boy, do I ever enjoy it when those times roll around! (The fried chicken is for breakfast on Mardi Gras, and fudge is always at Christmas.) For me, the best time for pecan pie is on Thanksgiving, along with pumpkin pie and maybe a cake. The only problem with that is that sometimes you eat too much turkey and trimmings to truly enjoy the dessert. So a smarter strategy would be to serve pecan pie after a very light meal to get the full effect. We are blessed with so many pecan trees in Louisiana that if you can beat the squirrels, you can pick up your ingredients in your own backyard. Another great thing about serving this on a holiday is that it is very easy to put together, especially if you use a ready-made crust. I like to keep a box of the rolled up frozen kind in my big freezer so that all you do is thaw it for a few minutes and your pie is on its way.

1 9-inch unbaked pie shell	½ tsp. salt
3 eggs	⅓ cup melted butter
2 tbsp. flour	1 tsp. vanilla extract
1 cup dark corn syrup	1 heaping cup pecan pieces
1 cup light brown sugar	

Preheat oven to 350 degrees. Bake pie shell for 5 minutes to set the crust.

In a medium bowl, beat eggs with a wire whisk until light and fluffy. Add flour, beating well. Add syrup, sugar, salt, butter, vanilla, and pecans and mix well.

Bake about 45 to 50 minutes until a toothpick inserted in the center comes out clean. Cool. Serve with whipped cream or vanilla ice cream, if desired.

Serves 6 to 8.

Praline Sauce

An excellent sauce to serve over ice cream, this makes great holiday gifts from your kitchen.

⅔ **cup water**
⅔ **cup light brown sugar, packed**
2 cups light corn syrup

2 tbsp. praline liqueur
2 tsp. vanilla extract
2 cups pecans, chopped

Combine all ingredients except pecans in a heavy pot. Bring just to a boil. Reduce heat and simmer for 5 minutes. Add pecans. Let cool and put in sterilized glass canning jars. Makes 5 half-pint jars.

Creamy Pralines

In my mind, two of the most frustrating recipes to make are fudge and pralines. Temperature is the key, of course. This is my most successful recipe for wonderful pralines that melt in your mouth.

1½ **cups light brown sugar**
1½ **cups granulated sugar**
1 cup evaporated milk
½ **tsp. cream of tartar**

⅛ **tsp. salt**
1 stick butter
2 tsp. vanilla
2½ **cups pecan halves**

Have a candy thermometer available. Lay out sheets of wax paper on a counter top. Have butter, vanilla, and pecan halves ready.

In a large saucepan, mix sugars, milk, cream of tartar, and salt. Mix thoroughly and heat over medium-high heat. Cook, stirring constantly, until temperature measures 240 degrees F on a candy thermometer. Remove from heat and immediately add butter, stirring. Add vanilla and whisk for a couple of minutes. Add pecans and continue to whisk until mixture begins to thicken. Drop quickly onto waxed paper by small spoonfuls. Cool until firm.

Makes about 50 2-inch pralines.

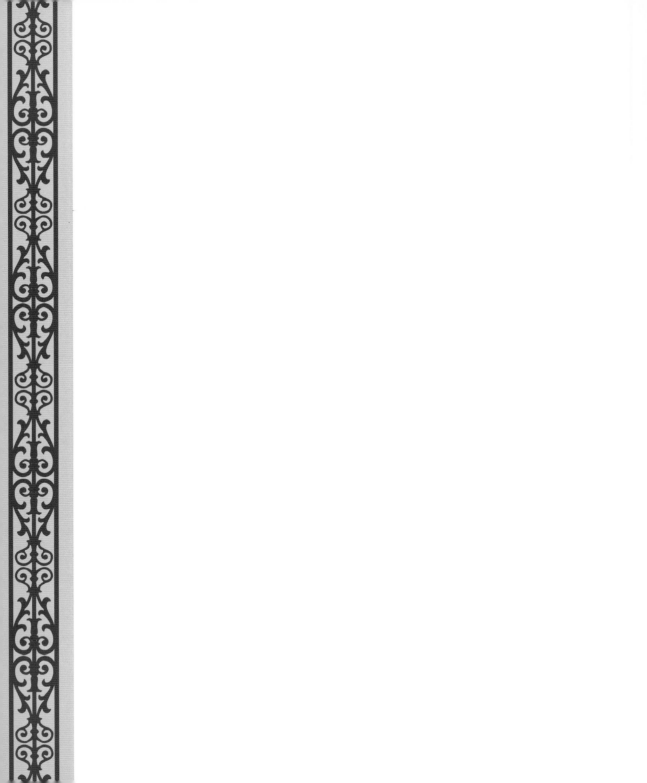

Index

7 Steaks in Gravy, 137

Alligator Sauce Piquant, 116
Asparagus with Hollandaise Sauce, 79

Baked Macaroni, 73
Baked Oysters, 114
Bananas Foster, 183
Barbecued Shrimp, 109
Beet Salad, 64
Belgian Endive with Crab Salad, 21
Boiled Beef, 138
Boiled Crabs, 91
Boudin, 142
Bourbon Sauce, 176
Bread Pudding, 175
Brie-crab Soup, 49
Brisket Stuffed with Crawfish Dressing, 139
Buttermilk Biscuits, 161

Cajun Rice Dressing, 72
Candied Sweet Potatoes, 77
Caramel Pie, 186
Cauliflower Salad, 65
Chargrilled Oysters, 27
Chicken and Andouille Gumbo, 59
Chicken and Dumplings, 126
Chicken Noodle Soup, 61
Chicken Sauce Piquant, 124
Corn and Shrimp Stew, 110
Corn Maque Choux, 89
Cornbread, 90
Crab Cakes, 92
Crab-stuffed Mushrooms, 20
Crawfish Bisque, 43
Crawfish Étouffée, 119

Crawfish Fettuccine, 118
Crawfish-stuffed Bread, 32
Creamed Potatoes with Horseradish, 84
Creamy Pralines, 189
Crème Brûlée, 179
Creole Daube, 132
Creole Meat Loaf, 135
Crêpes Fitzgerald, 184
Cup Custard, 177

Daube Glacé, 34
Deep-fried Turkey, 156
Drunken Chicken, 123

Eggplant Medallions with Crabmeat
    Béchamel, 97
Eggs Benedict, 168
Eggs Sardou, 167

Fig Cake, 169
Fig Preserves, 164
Fresh Blueberry Pie, 173
Fresh Tomato-herb Sauce for Pasta, 159
Fried Eggplant Fingers, 17

Garden Peas with Mushrooms and Pearl
    Onions, 81
Garlic Cheese Grits, 87
Grillades, 130
Grilled Pineapple, 185
Grilled Snapper, 105
Grits Soufflé, 86
Gumbo Z'herbes, 50

Hollandaise Sauce, 160
Hot Crab Dip, 22

Italian-style Cauliflower Soup, 58

Jambalaya, 120

Lemon Ice, 181
Liver and Onions, 152
Louisiana Bouillabaisse, 41
Louisiana Citrus Salad, 66

Marinated Crabs, 19

Natchitoches Meat Pies, 37
New Potatoes in Cream Sauce, 82

Old-fashioned Vanilla Custard Ice Cream,
    176
Oyster Dressing, 70
Oyster Pie, 115
Oyster-artichoke Soup, 46
Oysters Bienville, 23
Oysters Rockefeller, 24

Pain Perdu, 162
Pain Perdu with Berry Sauce, 163
Panéed Veal, 128
Pasta Milanese, 145
Pecan Pie, 188
Pecan-crusted Catfish, 102
Pork Chops and Noodles, 144
Pot Roast with Vegetables, 134
Potato Salad, 67
Potatoes au Gratin, Home-style, 83
Praline Sauce, 189
Pumpkin Bread, 165
Pumpkin Casserole, 76
Pumpkin Soup, 55

Red Beans and Rice, 150
Red Fish Courtbouillon, 104

Roast Duck, 153
Roasted Wild Ducks, 154
Rosemary Potatoes, 85

Sausage Balls, 33
Seafood Gumbo, 39
Seafood Lasagna, 117
Sesame-crusted Grilled Tuna, 103
Shrimp Creole, 111
Shrimp Po-Boy, 112
Shrimp Rémoulade, 29
Shrimp Wrapped in Bacon, 31
Shrimp-stuffed Avocados, 63
Smothered Chicken, 122
Snap Beans with New Potatoes, 75
Southern-style Greens, 80
Spaghetti and Meatballs, 140
Spinach-artichoke Soup, 57
Spinach-oyster Bake, 113
Standing Rib Roast, 136
Strawberry Custard Pie, 180
Strawberry Shortcake, 171
Strawberry-topped Cheesecake, 172
Stuffed Artichokes, 69
Stuffed Crabs, 95
Stuffed Eggplant, 98
Stuffed Mirlitons, 106
Stuffed Peppers, 149
Stuffed Whole Cabbage, 147

Trout Meunière, 99
Turtle Soup, 47

Veal Chops with Mushrooms and Marsala,
    129
Vegetable Soup, 52

White Bean Soup, 62
Whole Fish Creole, 101